ISLAND AT THE EDGE
OF THE WORLD

Also by Stephen Venables

PAINTED MOUNTAINS
EVEREST, KANGSHUNG FACE

ISLAND AT THE EDGE OF THE WORLD

A South Georgia Odyssey

STEPHEN VENABLES

Hodder & Stoughton
LONDON SYDNEY AUCKLAND TORONTO

BRITISH LIBRARY CATALOGUING-IN-PUBLICATION DATA

Venables, Stephen
  Island at the edge of the world: a South Georgia odyssey.
  I. Title
  919.7

  ISBN 0-340-55600-5

Published by Hodder and Stoughton,
a division of Hodder and Stoughton Ltd,
Mill Road, Dunton Green, Sevenoaks, Kent TN13 2YA.
Editorial Office: 47 Bedford Square, London WC1B 3DP.

Photoset by E.P.L. BookSet, Norwood, London.

Printed in Great Britain by St Edmundsbury Press,
Bury St Edmunds, Suffolk.

This book is dedicated to Duncan Carse,
whose mountain we climbed.

CONTENTS

MAPS

*All photographs, except where indicated,
are by the author, and courtesy of Kodak.*

Front of jacket photograph: King penguins on the
beach at Moltke Harbour, Royal Bay, late afternoon
on Christmas Day, 1989; back of jacket photograph:
Fur seal and blue-eyed Cormorant relaxing in Ocean
Harbour by the hulk of the *Bayard*, wrecked when
she ripped her moorings in 1911; black and white
photograph of the author by David Jones.

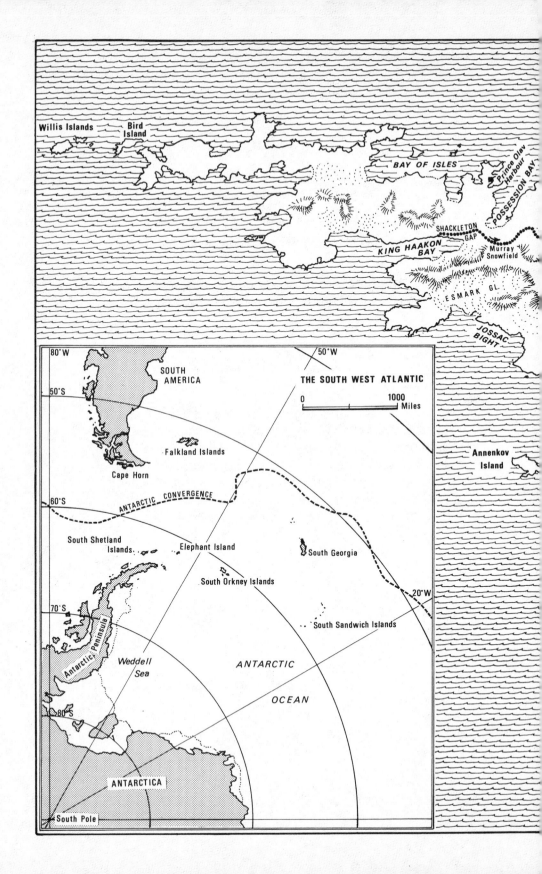

Willis Islands   Bird
                  Island

BAY OF ISLES

Prince Olav
Harbour

POSSESSION BAY

SHACKLETON
GAP

KING HAAKON
BAY

Murray
Snowfield

ESMARK GL.

JOSSAC
BIGHT

80°W

50°S

SOUTH
AMERICA

50°W

THE SOUTH WEST ATLANTIC

0   1000
                     Miles

Falkland Islands

Annenkov
Island

Cape Horn

ANTARCTIC CONVERGENCE

60°S

South Shetland
Islands

Elephant Island

South Georgia

South Orkney Islands

20°W

70°S

Antarctic Peninsula

Weddell
Sea

ANTARCTIC

South Sandwich Islands

OCEAN

80°S

ANTARCTICA

South Pole

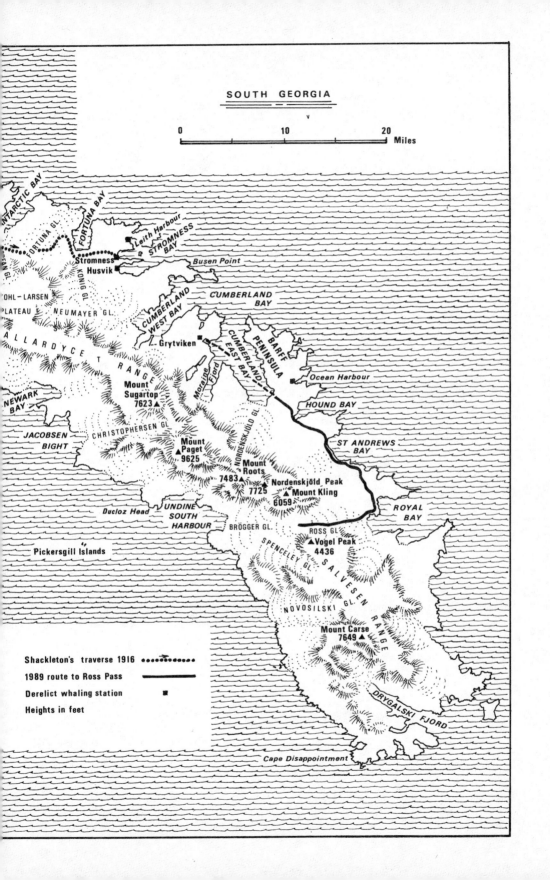

SOUTH GEORGIA

0   10   20
                              Miles

ANTARCTIC BAY

FORTUNA GL.
FORTUNA BAY

Leith Harbour
STROMNESS
BAY

Busen Point

Stromness
Husvik

KONG GL.

OHL-LARSEN
PLATEAU

NEUMAYER GL.

CUMBERLAND
WEST BAY

CUMBERLAND
BAY

ALLARDYCE T RANGE

Grytviken

CUMBERLAND
EAST BAY

BARFF
PENINSULA

Ocean Harbour

NEWARK
BAY

Mount
Sugartop
7623 ▲

Moraine Fjord

HOUND BAY

JACOBSEN
BIGHT

CHRISTOPHERSEN GL.

Mount
Paget
9625 ▲

NORDENSKJÖLD GL.

Mount
Roots

St ANDREWS
BAY

7483 ▲
7725 ▲

Nordenskjöld Peak
▲ Mount Kling
6059 ▲

Ducloz Head

UNDINE
SOUTH
HARBOUR

BRÖGGER GL.

ROSS GL.

ROYAL
BAY

Pickersgill Islands

SPENCELEY GL.

Vogel Peak
4436 ▲

SALVESEN RANGE

NOVOSILSKI GL.

Mount Carse
7649 ▲

DRYGALSKI
FJORD

Shackleton's traverse 1916 ●●●➔●●●●●

1989 route to Ross Pass ▬▬▬▬▬

Derelict whaling station ■

Heights in feet

Cape Disappointment

This book could not have been written without the expert advice of others who know far more than I about South Georgia. I would like particularly to thank Tom Arnbom, and John Croxall of the British Antarctic Survey, Nigel Bonner and Bob Headland, who gave me permission to quote from his definitive textbook on South Georgia and from William Barr's manuscript translation of *An Den Toren Der Antarktis* by Dr Ludwig Kohl-Larsen. Roger Perkins' *Operation Paraquat* was an invaluable source of information. I would also like to thank Nick Barker and Guy Sheridan, who gave me hours of their time to talk about the 1982 conflict, Patrick Fagan and Tony Bomford, who were amongst the island's most expert surveyors, Duncan Carse, who was an inexhaustible mine of information, and the BBC for permission to quote from Carse's radio script, 'Survival in Limbo'.

The decision to go to South Georgia was prompted largely by Julian Freeman-Attwood; I would like to thank him and the other expedition members, Brian Davison, Lindsay Griffin and Kees 't Hooft, for making it all possible; also Vivienne Schuster and my editor, Margaret Body; the book designer, Michael Clarke; and Alec Spark, who drew the maps. Most of all I want to thank my wife, Rosie, who gave me so much encouragement while I was writing the book.

SV

1

Shackleton's Island

I was flying down towards the sea, skimming the flaky swirls of snow. Knees juddered and ankles flexed instinctively, guiding my wayward skis so that I could hold my face up to the rushing air and stare ahead. Mountains were piled in massed tiers against the sky but the frozen sheet of glacier curved past, rolling down to fade into the endless blue expanse of the Southern Ocean, where random icebergs glinted in the sun.

I swerved and looked back to check that Brian was still following. Yes, he was still there, enjoying this glorious moment of speed on what was, this particular sunny morning, the world's greatest ski run – the Spenceley Glacier on the sub-Antarctic island of South Georgia. We had climbed our mountain and we were on our way home. Soon we would be back in the shelter of our snowcave. Tomorrow we would return to the coast, to rejoin the others at the hut, where there was plentiful food and whisky and tobacco. It would be good to see green grass again, to return to the call of the albatross and the penguins' bizarre trumpeting. I had even begun, during the past weeks on the glaciers, to miss the gross belching of the sea elephants.

The slope levelled out and my skis slid to a halt. Now I had to readjust bindings for walking on the level and head away from the island's west coast to a crucial pass that would lead us to the snowcave and the route back to the east coast.

Clouds began to drift across the glacier, obscuring the pass. I stopped to look at the map and take a compass bearing – almost due north – then continued, checking the compass every few minutes. But now the wind was blasting down from the peaks on the right, lashing my face with ice crystals, forcing me to cower and bend to the left whilst trying to push my skis forward on a steady course. Every few minutes I stopped to turn round and take a back bearing on Brian, just visible as a reassuring dark blob in the swirling white confusion.

After a mile the ground started to rise towards the pass and I stopped to wait. Brian arrived and shouted through the rising din: 'You've gone too far left. Give me the compass and I'll try to keep you on the right course.' So he directed me from behind as we pushed blindly up the slope, searching for the smooth snow saddle that would lead us between rocky pinnacles. A huge wind blast caught my top-heavy rucksack, knocking my body sideways, snapping boots out of the ski bindings and flinging me head first into the snow. I staggered back to my feet, cursing and fumbling with cold hands to refix ski bindings. A few yards further I was knocked over again. Behind me there was an angry scream as Brian went down, and more cursing as he fought to get his boots back into ski bindings. Again and again we were flung to the ground, shouting ourselves hoarse with filthy oaths. At one point I remembered the classic account of Scott's last Antarctic expedition, *The Worst Journey in the World*. Recalling the nightmarish winter journey, I shouted contemptuously, 'And that pompous sod Cherry-Garrard claimed they "never resorted to a single angry oath".'

Eventually we gave up the skis, strapped them to our rucksacks and fixed crampons to our boots. Now, with metal spikes on our feet, we had some purchase and just managed to climb the final slope to the crest of the ridge. But on the far side there was no smooth slope – just a vertical cliff dropping into the cloud.

'Where the hell are we?'

'Calm down,' Brian shouted. 'I think I can recognise this bit. We just need to head along this side of the ridge to the right.'

'All right, you show us the way.' But I failed to keep up with him, went off course and stumbled head first into a little hollow where all the winds of the Southern Ocean were funnelled into a malignant vortex.

After a long rest I stood up again, leaning at 45 degrees into the wind, bracing myself with outstretched ski poles. But I could see nothing through the ice film on my glasses so I had to sit down again and take them off. Now I could theoretically see something, even if it was just a myopic blur, but a thousand ice darts were stinging my unprotected eyeballs, forcing me to move with head bent sideways and one mitten held in front for protection, clawing my way out of the hollow like some drunken Quasimodo.

I managed a step, lifting my right foot forward and planting its metal spikes firmly into the ice to brace myself for the next blast. When the wind relented I moved my left foot forward. But on the third step I was caught out with one foot off the ground. The gust hit the skis on my rucksack, raised like sails above my head, and flung me back into the hollow. Several times I returned angrily to the fray, only to be repulsed; every time I took a step forward, I was thrown three steps back.

This was becoming ridiculous. Brian had vanished and here was I, the hero of Everest, the man who only eighteen months ago had descended alone through the storm from the world's highest summit, now pinned down at barely 2000 feet above sea level, stuck just a mile from shelter, completely unable to move and about to die of exposure. There was only one thing for it. I would have to crawl.

Brian, bless him, waited at the pass, eventually realised that something was wrong and came back to the rescue, moved to pity by the unutterable bathos of the great mountaineer, blind as a bat, helpless and disorientated, struggling on hands and knees through the blizzard. He grabbed me by the scruff of the neck, guided me out of the wind funnel, and soon we were safely over the pass.

It was quiet on the far side, with barely a hint of wind, but we still had to navigate our way through the final mile of cloud. Brian, for all his Antarctic mastery, was even less capable than I of walking in a straight line. So, as I followed with the compass, he was spurred on with shouts of 'Left . . . right . . . right a bit more . . . whoa, hold it there . . . no, back right a bit . . . too far . . . left a touch . . .'

After twenty minutes the impenetrable whiteness was broken by a dark blur which quickly materialised into the elegant curve where the glacier edge was scooped out below a rock cliff. Then the dark hairline of a marker wand confirmed that we were dead on target, safely back at the correct windscoop, the little hidden valley which had been our base during the past weeks. We left our skis stuck upright on the plateau and kicked steps down the wall of the scoop to a faint dent filled with quarried snow blocks. Brian pulled out the blocks to reveal a dark hole. He climbed into the hole and I passed over the two heavy rucksacks. Then I stepped through the doorway into the great blue cavern that was our base.

We were safely home; but the ridiculous struggle of the last two hours had been yet another reminder that on South Georgia you can take nothing for granted.

I was fifteen when I first became aware of South Georgia. It was 1969 and the long summer was almost over. I had survived the nuisance of 'O' Level exams and the bigger nuisance of a week's punishment, kept inside each hot afternoon as retribution for exploring the intricate Gothic rooftops of my school. The holidays had come and in August I had risen one morning at three o'clock to switch on the television and witness the strangely disappointing spectacle of Neil Armstrong taking man's first steps on the moon.

A few weeks later, staying with friends in Cornwall, I found a book which stirred infinitely deeper imaginings of exploration and adventure. The black cover was embossed with the silver outline of a three-masted sailing ship and beneath the elegant tracery of the ship's rigging, displayed in bold script, was the title, *South*, and the author's name, Shackleton. For the first time I read the extraordinary story of Ernest Shackleton's ill-fated attempt to make the first crossing of Antarctica.

The expedition ship, the *Endurance*, sailed from Plymouth in August 1914, just as Europe was engulfed by war. By January 1915 she was 10,000 miles south, fighting her way through the pack ice of the Weddell Sea. Then, within sight of the Antarctic coastline, the ship became trapped in the ice and started to drift inexorably back north, away from the continent Shackleton had set his heart on crossing. Month after month the vessel moved slowly north with the ice until unbearable pressures started to crush the hull, forcing the expedition to abandon ship and camp on the ice. On November 21st, 1915 the *Endurance* sank, leaving twenty-eight men stranded on the ice with just the three tiny ship's boats, sledges, tents and dwindling reserves of food and fuel.

'Ice Camp' drifted north for another four months until finally the ice started to break up and the men were forced to take to the boats. They had now drifted past the Antarctic Peninsula and in desperation they headed for the bleak, uninhabited shore of Elephant Island. Three days later, when the drenched, frostbitten, exhausted men dragged the boats up on to the boulder beach, it was the first land they had touched for sixteen months but it brought little solace. Their rations were fast running out and would have to be supplemented by penguin meat and blubber. Another winter was drawing in. No one else in the world knew of their plight and they were separated from the nearest habitation by the vast storm-swept tracts of the Southern Ocean.

Shackleton, having got his men this far, could so easily have succumbed to despair, but he started immediately to prepare the toughest of the three tiny boats for a desperate voyage. In the prevailing westerly winds there was no chance of reaching South America or the Falkland Islands to the north; but by sailing 850 miles north-east he might just reach one of the whaling stations on South Georgia and summon help. It was a desperate bid – setting sail with five companions in a 22-foot open boat, to navigate the world's stormiest ocean, knowing that if they missed the tiny island of South Georgia they would drift on across the Atlantic until they died, leaving no hope for the other twenty-two men marooned on Elephant Island.

The voyage lasted sixteen days. During the night of the twelfth day the boat was hit by the biggest wave Shackleton had ever seen during all his years as a merchant seaman and his three voyages to Antarctica. Yet the tiny boat, with its flimsy improvised canvas decking, survived to give the men further days of unmitigated suffering. Each four-hour watch was a miserable battle to bale out the constant floods, man rudder and sails and scrape ice from the decking. 'Below deck' the three men off watch cowered under the canvas, either dozing or trying to work the primus stove amidst a sodden lurching chaos of moulting reindeer sleeping bags, spilt paraffin, salt encrusted food and the angular boulders they carried for ballast. By the end of the voyage the men were down to a quarter of a pint of brackish water each a day and were tormented by a burning salty thirst.

The voyage of the *James Caird* was one of the most remarkable stories in the annals of the sea, but when Shackleton and his five men finally beached their flimsy craft on the shore of South Georgia the journey was not over. They had landed on the desolate south-west coast of the island and the nearest whaling station was seventeen miles away as the crow flies, on the more sheltered north-east coast. The scrap of a chart they had depicted only the coastline, inaccurately at that, and in 1916 no one had really penetrated South Georgia's interior of jagged mountains and unmapped glaciers.

Three men stayed with the boat. Shackleton and the other two set off with three days' iron rations, fifty feet of knotted rope and a carpenter's adze. They travelled non-stop, taking thirty-six hours to find their way across nearly thirty miles of uncharted, heavily crevassed glaciers, complex mountain ridges and steep ice slopes, frequently having to retrace their steps when faced with impossible cliffs. Even now, with accurate maps, a fresh, well-equipped team of experienced mountaineers would be pushed to equal their speed over that terrain; in 1916, exhausted after the horrendous boat journey, Shackleton's crossing of the island was a brilliant feat of intuitive mountaineering.

Fifty-three years after the first crossing of South Georgia, I read Shackleton's account of the wonderful moment when he heard the factory siren at Stromness whaling station and knew that his trial was almost over. I still get a lump in the throat every time I re-read the passage where the three filthy, blackened men reach the whaling station and have to explain to the incredulous manager that they are the same men who sailed south in the *Endurance* eighteen months earlier. The most moving moment of all comes later, after three rescue attempts from South Georgia, the Falklands and Chile have been thwarted by pack ice, when Shackleton finally gets through with a ship on the fourth attempt and rescues the twenty-two men marooned on Elephant Island, reduced after four months to a diet of limpets.

Like any impressionable fifteen-year-old, I was stirred by a story of obstinate courage, charismatic leadership and survival against all odds. Sitting in that comfortable house beside the tame Cornish estuary in 1969, I was also moved by the savage landscape in

6

which Shackleton's drama unfolded. I scrutinised Frank Hurley's masterly black and white photographs of the ship beset in the ice, the desolate cliffs of Elephant Island and, most grand of all, the great mountain ranges of South Georgia. I had already seen glaciated mountains for myself, in the Swiss Alps, but nothing to match these untamed Antarctic peaks with their immense glaciers tumbling headlong into the sea. Perhaps it was that combination of mountains and sea that made such a deep impression – that and the photographs of the sea elephants lolling on the storm-swept beaches.

At that stage I hardly imagined that I might see South Georgia for myself. Later I began to climb in Wales and Scotland and the Alps, gaining some competence as a mountaineer and opening up the possibility of adventures further afield. In 1977 I travelled with four friends to the Hindu Kush range in Afghanistan, starting a long series of Himalayan expeditions that were increasingly to dominate my life, resulting in haphazard employment and the eternally unresolved conflict between a love of adventure and the niggling desire for a life of secure creative domesticity.

In the Seventies and Eighties travel became easier and cheaper than ever before. I watched the condors circling the high Andes of Bolivia, trudged through the high altitude forests of Uganda, climbed virgin peaks in Kashmir, trekked across Snow Lake and visited the great plateau of Tibet. But Antarctica retained some of its exclusive mystique – remote and extremely expensive, it seemed, unless someone would pay you to go there. In 1978 I applied for a job with the British Antarctic Survey. The post of general assistant in these days of motor sledges seems to require a natural affinity with two-stroke petrol engines and I was not accepted. However, during the sudden flush of hopeful enthusiasm before the interview, I read widely about the great southern continent and its surrounding oceans. I became more aware of the beauty and fragility of its unique ecology and of the Utopian international Antarctic Treaty, which aims to protect the only continent that has no indigenous human population. A friend introduced me to his father, who had been captain of the patrol vessel, HMS *Protector*. He talked nostalgically about the long months amongst the icebergs and laughed at the absurdity of being there to help support the peaceful scientific interests of the British Antarctic bases, whilst keeping a territorial eye on the Argentinians. An uneasy truce existed on the Antarctic mainland, where all territorial claims are frozen by the treaty, but just north of the 60th parallel, outside the treaty area, several islands including South Georgia were claimed as British sovereign territory.

I was working in York in March 1982 when the first reports came through of an unauthorised Argentinian landing on South Georgia to collect scrap metal from one of the deserted whaling stations. With even my limited knowledge of the area, it came as no surprise when the 'salvage men' moved on to the administrative base at King Edward Point, overwhelmed the tiny garrison and hoisted the Argentinian flag. Recalling Frank Hurley's photographs of the wild glaciated coastline, I was suitably impressed at the task facing the British forces sent to retake the island in the southern winter.

After the Falklands conflict the British government decided to maintain a permanent garrison on South Georgia. One of the first garrison commanders to do his four-month tour at King Edward Point was Captain Nigel Williams, a keen mountaineer. I met him in 1987 when we both took part in a joint civil–military expedition to Shisha Pangma, the world's thirteenth highest mountain, in Tibet. The expedition assembled in the Nepalese capital, Kathmandu, and it was here, roaming the hot crowded bazaar in search of cooking pots, that Nigel told me, incongruously, about his time on South Georgia. 'It was a bit frustrating: I had nearly forty men under my command, mainly very young, with virtually no experience. Most of the time we had to be manning the base, and even on patrols we couldn't travel far. And yet there are over a hundred different glaciers, some of them unexplored ... and all those unclimbed peaks.'

His enthusiasm added another patch of colour to my hazy picture of the island and, perhaps, the subconscious decision that one day I would see the place for myself. During that expedition to Tibet, with its masonic undercurrent of tribal military connections, there were other influences and coincidences at work. I met Colonel John Blashford-Snell, the magician who had found the sponsorship to pay for this expedition and was later to provide a vital contact in the Royal Navy. There was the climber with military connections who muttered about the possibility of 'jacking up' a trip to South Georgia one day. And there was Caradoc Jones, the utterly civilian itinerant Welshman who never actually reached Tibet because, on the way home from Peru and Chile, he had made a detour to the Falkland Islands where he got a job with the fisheries board, researching the South Atlantic squid population. He too, in his postcards, was muttering things about South Georgia.

The Welsh squid-sexer's failure to reach Kathmandu left a vacancy which was filled at the last minute by one Julian Freeman-Attwood. Our paths had almost crossed the previous Christmas when we were each independently climbing the three highest peaks of East Africa. Later that year he had telephoned to say he wanted to come and ask about good places to visit in the Himalaya. At that time I was repainting the house where I lodged in London, to pay my rent, and I was busy at the top of a ladder when a diesel pick-up chugged to a halt in the street below and a sketchily shaved man in rustic hat walked up to the house. I stared down at the country yokel. He stared back at the paint-spattered workman and asked whether Stephen Venables was in the house. 'Yes, it's me. I'll come down and get us some lunch.'

Wine, bread, cheese and olives were despatched with the abstraction of a man accustomed to having meals placed in front of him and dirty dishes spirited magically away afterwards. All the while he talked, with a slightly manic look in the blue eyes, about his uncle's Shropshire estate where he lived and worked as a forester, and about the mountain ranges he wanted to visit, occasionally stabbing a gnarled finger at some area of the map and firing a question at the Himalayan expert. I remained suitably reticent as this complete stranger dreamed his way aloud across the world's greatest range of mountains, throwing in the odd supplementary reference to Africa, Scotland or Antarctica.

After lunch we looked at some slides; then I returned to work and the whirlwind shot off back to Shropshire. Now in his mid-thirties, he had come late to mountains and was clearly making up for lost time. So, three months later, when he suddenly received a phone call from Kathmandu inviting him at five days' notice to join an expedition to one of the world's highest mountains, he came without hesitation.

The expedition had already left Kathmandu and we were at the Tibetan border post when an old truck drove up and Julian leapt out of the back, like some Indiana Jones understudy in tweed and trilby, hot on the trail of adventure. Perhaps he was disappointed, for during the six weeks of the attempt on Shisha Pangma he was confined most of the time to the drudgery of load-carrying. I was one of the lucky ones up in front, pushing out the route, and I only met Julian three times during the whole expedition. However, our brief encounters were friendly and we kept in touch after the expedition.

A few months later I was in the Himalaya again, climbing a new route on Everest. Recovering in Kathmandu after making the first British ascent of the world's highest mountain without bottled oxygen, I enjoyed my brief moment of fame and glory, answering a barrage of telephone calls from the London press. One evening I spoke to a reporter at *The Times*, Boris Johnson, who enthused down the telephone in fruity tones, 'Gosh. Fantastic. Sooper dooper. It's absolutely spiffing,' like some P. G. Wodehouse museum piece. A few minutes later there was a call from deepest Shropshire: 'Hello, it's Julian. Did you speak to Boris . . . ? Yes . . . he's my cousin. Congratulations. Some of the Shisha Pangma lot are here and we're all thrilled.'

I was touched by the phone call and later that year, back in England, I went with my girlfriend, Rosie, to stay at Julian's cottage in Shropshire. There was something very seductive about the place, waking up in the morning to look out through oak window frames past a tangle of climbing roses to dewy fields and woods, or sitting in the evening round a gigantic wood fire, drinking wine and enjoying pheasant or venison, exquisitely cooked by Julian's girlfriend, Elaine. In the Seventies he had found the house abandoned on his uncle's estate, occupied only by cows, had evicted them, removed tons of dung and, over the years, turned the place into a delightful base without resorting to the vandalism of 'home improvement'. For someone so obsessed with travel he had unusually strong roots and a deep sense of belonging to his particular patch of the earth.

Julian's education was sketchy. He hated Eton and left at sixteen to live with his mother in London and 'attend 'A' Level courses' at Holland Park Comprehensive, then in its liberal heyday. I never discovered what subjects he was supposed to have studied, but it seemed that the students' alternative curriculum of wild partying had left a deeper impression. After leaving school he moved to Shropshire, enjoying the carefree life of an aristocratic country bumpkin. Piecing together his random reminiscences, I filled in a kaleidoscopic picture of farm labouring, lorry driving, rabbit shooting, illegal speeding in battered old cars, grand weekend parties with famous rock musicians, eccentric relations, masterful butlers, journeys in a gypsy caravan ... all remembered nostalgically through a distant haze of marijuana smoke.

Somewhere along the line two themes emerged. One was a passionate interest in conservation and his decision to earn his living as a forester. The other was travel. In 1981 he joined Quentin Crewe's overland expedition to the Sahara. Later he bought a part share in *Baroque*, the pilot cutter which had been sailed to the ends of the earth by H. W. Tilman. And so he became a Tilman fan, avidly reading all the great explorer's books and discovering, through Tilman's wry prose, the magic of wild mountainous country. By the time I met Julian he had some good mountaineering experience and was already, like most of us, dreaming of Antarctica, Patagonia and the mountainous islands of the Southern Ocean. At the end of 1989 we discussed the possibility of an expedition to South Georgia.

It was John Blashford-Snell, the pith-helmeted veteran of the Darien Gap and the Blue Nile, who made the dream a possibility. During the Shisha Pangma expedition he had taken to Julian and later asked whether he might get involved with one of his Operation Raleigh youth expeditions to Chile. Julian asked if I was also interested but, much as I admired John's work, I did not see myself as a leader of massed intrepid youth. However, John had occasionally extended his formidable powers of influence to help undeserving hacks well beyond the first flush of youth. He clearly liked Julian and he had said very nice things about me in the press. Perhaps we could go somewhere more remote ... do a reconnaissance for Operation Raleigh? What about South Georgia?

Julian said he would suggest the idea, although the chances of John enabling us to reach that remote island seemed pretty slim. Just before Christmas, Julian received a postcard suggesting that John might be able to help. Then, early in January 1989, he telephoned excitedly to ask, 'Can you come to a meeting with Blashers and his friend, Alan Marr? He has a fishing fleet down in the South Atlantic and can probably help. It looks as though we're going to South Georgia.'

2

Corridors of Power

Alan Marr had no ships available, but both he and John were keen on the project and had other contacts up their sleeves, so we left the meeting in good spirits. We had decided that we were going to visit South Georgia during the southern summer of 1989–90, and once you decide something like that it usually happens. We had just ten months to organise the trip and during that time I began to find out more about South Georgia, padding out the romantic image of Shackleton's desolate mountainous island with some hard fact.

Captain James Cook made the first recorded landing on South Georgia in 1775, when he sailed south in *Resolution* on his second great voyage of exploration, in search of the still unknown 'Southern Continent'. He landed in Possession Bay, 'displayed our colours and took possession of the country in his Majesty's name [George III] under a discharge of small Arms'. In his log he described the perpendicular face of a glacier, disgorging great icebergs into the bay, and continued: 'The inner parts of the Country was not less savage and horrible: the Wild rocks raised their lofty summits till they were lost in the Clouds and the Vallies laid buried in everlasting Snow. Not a tree or shrub was to be seen, no not even big enough to make a toothpick.'

Cook explored and charted the intricate bays and headlands along the east coast until he rounded Cape Disappointment, the southern point of what proved to be a crescent-shaped island about a hundred miles long, not the great continent he had hoped to find. The Antarctic mainland is in fact several hundred miles further south, but South Georgia lies within the limit of the Antarctic ocean currents, hence the comparatively cold climate for an island only at the equivalent latitude of Edinburgh.

The dynamics of the Southern Ocean are complex but, put very simply, Antarctica, because it is a vast continent, affects a much greater area of ocean in the south than the Arctic floating ice sheet does in the north. As the massive ice barriers around the continent melt they cool the surrounding ocean. This melting, combined with huge precipitation in the area, also dilutes the salt content of the water. So Antarctica is surrounded by a great mass of cold de-salinated water tending to flow northwards. There comes a point where this cold flow meets warmer water flowing south from the Indian, Pacific and Atlantic oceans, but there is very little mingling of the currents because the desalinated water, heavier than the warm salty water it meets, sinks underneath. Instead of a gradual shift of temperature, there is an abrupt climatic change where the two masses of water meet. This meeting point is called the Antarctic Convergence.

It might be assumed that the Antarctic Convergence forms a precise circle around Antarctica, following an exact line of latitude. In fact it weaves an erratic line, sometimes as far north as the Forties, sometimes further south than 60 degrees. In the South-West Atlantic the Convergence slants up from the south of Cape Horn, between the Falklands and South Georgia, before circling east at approximately 50 degrees. South Georgia is virtually on the same latitude as the Falklands, but because it lies within the Convergence the climate is much colder.

The climate is governed by the sea and by the wind – the wind which circles Antarctica clockwise, screaming relentlessly round the Southern Ocean. As Wally Herbert, the distinguished polar explorer wrote: 'The weather conditions on the sub-Antarctic islands are appalling at all seasons of the year. Every kind of precipitation falls or lashes the glaciated slopes and a shroud of fog or dank overcast persists for much of the year. Gales and storms tear at the surface . . . ' Two hundred years earlier one of the naturalists aboard Cook's ship suggested: 'If a Captain, some Officers and a Crew were convicted of some heinous crimes, they ought to be sent by way of punishment to these inhospitable cursed Regions, for to explore and survey them. The very thought to live here a year fills the whole Soul with horror and despair.

God! what miserable wretches must they be, that live here in these terrible Climates!'

The disenchanted naturalist, George Forster, was seeing South Georgia in 1775 when Wordsworth was only five. The Romantic Movement had not begun and the notion hardly existed that wild scenery could be ennobling and uplifting. However, he did note the teeming wildlife on and around the island, for it was already evident that the cold waters of the Southern Ocean, far from being a desert, supported a rich profusion of marine life. Now we know that cold sea water is richer in nitrogenous compounds than temperate and tropical waters, providing the ideal breeding ground for the plankton which nourish the krill, which, in turn, form the basis of the entire Antarctic food chain.

Forster recorded the huge numbers of penguins, petrels, seals and whales in the bays and on the cliffs and beaches of South Georgia; but his account is coloured less with a sense of wonder than calculations about possible commercial exploitation. He predicted that it could be a very long time before depletion of whale and seal stocks further north tempted any hunter to suffer the dangers and hardships of the bleak sub-Antarctic islands he disliked so much. But only eleven years later, in 1786, the first seals were taken from South Georgia and in the following years British, Norwegian and particularly American sealers ravaged the island's population. Elephant seals were killed for their blubber, which could be rendered down to valuable oil, but the real prize was the fur seal. During a record catch in the 1800–01 season a sealer from New York killed 57,000 fur seals before sailing with the pelts to China, where there was a big demand from the felted fur trade.

Sealing was the motivation for many of the early Antarctic voyages of exploration and perhaps the most celebrated explorer was James Weddell, who recorded during his voyage of 1822–4 that 'the number of skins brought off South Georgia by ourselves and foreigners cannot be estimated at fewer than 1,200,000 . . . these animals are [already] almost extinct.' Elephant seal stocks were not quite so badly depleted and during the twentieth century they revived to support quite a profitable industry, controlled by stringent quotas. However, that later phase of sealing was run on the back of the infinitely more profitable whaling operation.

The invention of the harpoon gun in 1865 began the transformation of whaling into an efficient mechanised industry equipped to fulfil the prophecies of George Forster. By the turn of the century northern stocks had dwindled drastically and the whalers looked to the teeming Southern Ocean. The lee coast of South Georgia, with its ice-free natural harbours and unlimited freshwater supplies, was the perfect base for operations in Antarctica. The Norwegian explorer and entrepreneur, Carl Anton Larsen, established the first whaling station at Grytviken in 1904 and soon other stations were built on the island. At first the operation was highly profitable – shareholders in Larsen's Compañía Argentina de Pesca, registered in Buenos Aires, saw their dividends increase by up to 500 per cent a year – but later attempts to conserve stocks were hopelessly inadequate. By 1965, when depletion of southern stocks rendered the industry uneconomical, 175,000 whales had been processed on South Georgia, out of a total of 1,500,000 taken from Antarctica.

Ever since Cook's discovery in 1775 Britain had claimed sovereignty over South Georgia, and when commercial whaling started on the island the various companies had to apply to the Falklands government for leases. In 1909 a permanent Magistrate was appointed and an administrative post established at King Edward Point, a small spit of flat land just across the cove from Grytviken. From that year the island was administered peacefully from King Edward Point until it was attacked and occupied by Argentinian soldiers in 1982.

Over the years Argentina had made repeated claims to South Georgia and the rest of the Falkland Island Dependencies, but things came to a head in February 1982 when the Argentinian businessman Sir Constantino Davidoff, who had a contract to salvage machinery and scrap metal from the defunct whaling stations, landed at Leith Harbour without first requesting permission from the Magistrate at King Edward Point, twelve miles away. During the following weeks more Argentinian ships arrived, the Argentinian flag was flown at Leith and a military build-up culminated in the attack on King Edward Point on April 3rd.

Three weeks later King Edward Point was retaken by British forces. Throughout the crisis a key role was played by HMS

Endurance, the ice patrol vessel named after Shackleton's historic ship. Since 1968 HMS *Endurance* had been the symbol of Britain's involvement in the South Atlantic and, ironically, the decision a few weeks earlier by Margaret Thatcher and the Defence Secretary, John Nott, to scrap the ship at the end of the 1981–2 southern summer had been one of the signals encouraging Argentina to invade South Georgia and the Falklands. The Foreign Secretary, Lord Carrington, had repeatedly urged his colleagues to reconsider and for months the ship's commanding officer, Captain Nicholas Barker, had been warning the government of an impending Argentinian attack; but Britain, in time-honoured tradition, waited until the invasion had actually happened before responding.

After the 1982 conflict Nicholas Barker was belatedly and rather grudgingly awarded the CBE. He spent a year at Cambridge researching his own report on the future of the South Atlantic and later took command of the brand new HMS *Sheffield* that replaced the ship sunk off the Falklands. The *Endurance* was kept in service and has continued each year to make her long southern tour, flying the flag at South American ports, the Falklands, South Georgia, the South Sandwich Islands and the British Antarctic Survey bases on the mainland, in her ambivalent mixture of roles, part military, part diplomatic, part scientific.

It has always been a tradition with the *Endurance* to take some civilian passengers south. Early in 1989, when Julian and I were looking for transport to South Georgia and realising that Alan Marr's fishing boats could not help, John Blashford-Snell kindly introduced us to his friend Nicholas Barker, in the hope that he might be able to persuade the current captain of the *Endurance* to help us.

We arranged to visit Captain Barker at his Northumberland home in March, on the way back from a trip to Scotland. It was only nine months after my Everest climb and I was still busy with a full timetable of lectures and media appearances. That week I was scheduled to take the *Blue Peter* presenter, Karen Keating, ice climbing on Ben Nevis, but bad weather delayed the climb for a day. Julian stayed on to watch some hilarious filming and look after the BBC safety officer; then, as the weather closed in again and the spindrift avalanches started to pour down on the assembled throng of cameramen and production assistants, we were whisked off in a helicopter to our getaway car. We were now a day behind schedule and I was due to lecture in Keswick, so Julian went alone to see Captain Barker. Two days later he phoned me to confirm that the captain was strongly recommending the current *Endurance* management to give us a lift south the following December.

After the expedition I went to visit Nick Barker myself and asked him just why he had offered so generously to help a party of civilian strangers. He told me how he had got the command of HMS *Endurance* as his first captain's job. 'At the time I had virtually no idea what she did. So I spent some time at the Foreign and Commonwealth Office, and in Cambridge I talked to the people at the British Antarctic Survey and Scott Polar Research Institute and realised that this was going to be the most fascinating job . . . and it was! By far the most interesting part, from my point of view, was the ship's scientific role.'

During his two seasons of command he gave lifts south to David Attenborough, who 'wanted to look at some penguins in the South Sandwich Islands' and Monica Christensen, the Norwegian polar scientist and explorer. 'Everyone on the ship was in tears when we said goodbye to her.' He also helped Joint Services expeditions to South Georgia and Brabant Island. At the end of the 1982 battle one of his last jobs was to take on board a crate containing two South Georgia pintails bound for Peter Scott's wildlife sanctuary, 8000 miles away at Slimbridge. 'I was always delighted to help anyone we could. Just after you met Alan Marr, I was on a shoot here with him and John Blashford-Snell and they asked if I could do anything.' So early in 1989 he wrote to his latest successor on the *Endurance*, recommending the Southern Ocean Mountaineering Expedition for a lift to South Georgia.

A colonel who has spent a good part of his career organising services expeditions to the Himalaya once told me that anything is possible with the British Armed Services if you know how to play the system. With our commendation from Nicholas Barker we imagined innocently that we, undeserving civilians, were playing the system successfully, but as the hot summer of 1989 wore on we realised that nothing had actually been agreed. We had, for the purposes of sponsorship, brazenly produced a prospectus announcing that after flying to the Falklands we would be sailing with the *Endurance* to South Georgia, but no one had confirmed our lift, let alone transport back from the island. Things came to a head in July while Julian was away on holiday and I was manning the telephone. After several attempts I got through on the telephone to Portsmouth where a new captain, Norman Hodgson, had just taken over command of the *Endurance*.

I had been warned that 'Stormy Norm' was not always sweetness and light, so I tried the deferential approach. The first time we spoke he was quite prickly, but when I phoned again later he apologised: 'I'm sorry I was a bit abrupt with you, but Nick Barker dealt with my predecessor who never explained who you were or why on earth I should take you to South Georgia. We're very tight for space this year, but we can probably squeeze you in once you've flown down to the Falklands. How many of you are there?'

'A minimum of four, but if you could manage six . . . '

'If you can stick to five, my job will be a lot easier. And you've got to arrange for someone to get you off the island – your prospectus claims that the *Endurance* will pick you up. I don't know where you got that idea from: we're not calling at South Georgia after December.'

I grovelled down the telephone and he continued, 'I have a very busy workload and I haven't got time to come and pick you up if something goes wrong. So I'm afraid unless you can prove how you're going to get home, I can't take you there in the first place. And you must get clearance from the Commanding Officer in the Falklands and the Governor.'

I embarked on a desperate telephone campaign, trying Alan Marr again, calling the Falklands Office in London, getting satellite relay to ship owners in Port Stanley and, back in London, pestering an unending list of civil servants, who handed me from telephone extension to extension down the labyrinthine corridors of Whitehall. After a hard day's talking I had got nowhere and, in despair, I telephoned Operation Raleigh and eventually tracked down our patron 'Blashers', who, after a lifetime's employment in the British Army, warned, 'Steer clear of bureaucracy. Better to go direct.' He couldn't help with our return transport but agreed to write immediately to the Falklands Governor to seek formal permission for our expedition.

The telephone campaign continued as I racked my brains for strings to pull. I phoned a retired MOD friend of my parents, whose next-door neighbour was a retired admiral. He put me on to a new set of Whitehall numbers and eventually the Royal Fleet Auxiliary, where an official confirmed that a ship might be calling at South Georgia in March and gave me the address to write to. Then I remembered Douggie Keelan, the Royal Marines colonel whom I had last met in Kathmandu on the way to Everest. A friend found me his number and warned me to phone quickly as Douggie was about to disappear on some clandestine mission.

Douggie saved us. 'Yes – shouldn't be a problem, a good mate of mine is just taking over as Commander of British Forces in the Falkland Islands. Present chap is RAF and they wouldn't help anyone, but my Royal Marines chum, Paul Stevenson, is taking over next month. I'll send him a signal.'

Two days later Douggie showed me a rough draft. 'General Stevenson – CBFFI . . . Request permission for mountaineering expedition . . . Venables of Everest fame . . . whole team highly competent . . . bona fides beyond reproach . . . outward transport in HMS *Endurance* . . . hoping for return passage with RFA . . . ' And so it went on, putting an authoritative military gloss on our suspect civilian venture.

By the time Julian returned from the Dolomites I was able to assure him that the expedition now looked much more likely to happen. By the end of July we would know definitely.

Then on July 25th a letter from the Ministry of Defence nearly scuppered the whole project. This particular interference had been caused entirely by my misjudgment. Earlier in the year I had attended an official drinks party at 10 Downing Street, where I had told the Prime Minister about our proposed expedition. That same busy week I joined assorted survivors of hijacks, train crashes and other disasters, to receive a Gold Medal from that acme of sensitive journalism, the *Daily Star*. The ceremony, com-

plete with video flashbacks, exploited disaster with cloying senti-
mentality and the final scene, when everyone stood up to applaud
while the Prime Minister herself was awarded a special Gold Star
to the accompaniment of 'Land of Hope of Glory', seemed a little
overstated. However, that was hardly her fault and, jingoism
aside, I felt very flattered when my turn came, as the token
adventurer, to receive my medal. She remembered exactly who I
was and shouted out to all the bemused journalists: 'He's climbed
Everest and now he's off to climb in South Georgia.'

On the basis of this enthusiasm we wrote to ask Margaret
Thatcher if she would be official patron of the expedition, hoping
naively that with her endorsement all doors would be opened. We
were not really surprised, though, when the Prime Minister's
private secretary replied that, regretfully, she would have to say
'no' as she received so many requests of this nature. More alarm-
ingly, she was concerned that if anything went wrong we might
prove a burden to the fully stretched defence forces in the South
Atlantic, so she had written to the Ministry of Defence to inform
them of our plans.

Now, several weeks later, just as we were getting everything
sewn up, my brief flirtation in the corridors of power backfired
with a weighty letter from the MOD. The indigestible reference
number was ominous – D/Sec (0)(C)10/6/17/3 – and the letter
itself listed several reasons why we should not visit South Georgia,
concluding:

The search and rescue problem, however, is the fundamental
one, and I am afraid that for the reasons outlined above we
would need to be satisfied that you had some alternative source
of emergency cover before we could agree to support your
expedition with transport to and from South Georgia.

I am sorry to be sending you what you are likely to regard as
an unhelpful letter, but I hope you will be able to appreciate our
problem.

Yours sincerely
Norman Abbott

I retaliated immediately with a long missive bristling with

influential names, contingency plans and a rather pompous dismissal of the official ethos of referred responsibility:

> Your most serious concern is about the 'search and rescue problem'. As a group of highly competent mountaineers with a combined experience of over fifty years operating in remote uninhabited regions we do not perceive this to be a problem . . . when I was climbing a new route up the biggest, hardest face of Everest last year, there was not the remotest chance of a rescue . . . when Julian Freeman-Attwood crossed the Sahara etc. etc. If help were available we would obviously accept it gratefully and pay any bills, but we would not dream of demanding or expecting help as our right: that would be complete anathema to experienced moutaineers.

Mr Abbott was, of course, only doing his job and we admitted privately that he had a right to be worried. Luckily my letter, and another from Julian emphasising the extent of our insurance, seemed to convince him that our expedition was competently organised and would be completely self-sufficient on the island, for when we next heard from Mr Abbott it was to offer us 'best wishes for a successful expedition'. By that time General Stevenson had generously agreed to sanction the civilian intruders and take ultimate responsibility for us, promising that we could probably have a lift from South Georgia back to the Falklands during March 1990 in a Royal Fleet Auxiliary vessel. With that assurance in place, Captain Hodgson agreed to take our ton and a half of gear and supplies south when the *Endurance* sailed in early November. We would fly out a month later to the Falklands and meet the ship there for the final 850-mile sea passage to South Georgia. Through a mixture of obstinacy, luck and shameless exploitation of personal contacts, we had finally succeeded in playing the system.

Now that the expedition was definite we had to finalise the team. During the 1987 Tibet expedition Julian had befriended an amiable giant called Lindsay Griffin and two years later he was still reminiscing fondly about the Great Tibetan Storm, when he had battled back to base camp with Lindsay and the rest of their group, floundering through the worst blizzard in living memory. Time after time, six and a half feet of Griffin had disappeared into snow drifts and concealed crevasses, and it had taken the combined strength of Julian and the others to haul him, foot by foot, back to the surface.

I first met Lindsay closer to home, on the Mer de Glace near Mont Blanc. It was 1975 and I had just left Oxford. Lindsay had graduated a few years earlier but his name was still uttered with reverence amongst Oxford climbers. He had recently made a desperate retreat from near the top of Mont Blanc, only just escaping the winter blizzard alive, leaving impressionable strangers with an image of a rugged man in the heroic mould. But here, gangling across the ice like some great stork, limping slightly from frostbite injuries and burdened with an overloaded rucksack, was a creature that seemed expressly designed to malfunction in the mountains. The heroic image was further squashed by shoulder-length reddish hair, home-made clothes and a gentle manner when we asked him if he knew the correct approach to our mountain. He didn't but was very friendly – genial, polite and firmly secretive about his own plans.

Later during that summer at Chamonix I began to chip away at the wall of secrecy and get to know him. We did a route together and returned to the Alps the following year to climb in winter. In 1977 it was with Lindsay and three others that I made my first expedition to Afghanistan. In later years we often met at his home in North Wales, we visited Bolivia together and in 1987 we were both on the Tibet expedition.

Meanwhile two serious accidents had left Lindsay permanently injured, with one leg shorter than the other, but he continued stoically to climb his way around the world. On one occasion he was still on crutches when he limped to the summit of Mexico's volcano, Cotapapetl. His determination seemed to border on monomania and to someone like me, who is really happiest staying at home, that all-consuming passion for mountains was hard to comprehend. However, his obsession was redeemed by a refreshing absence of ambition and he seemed less concerned with fame and glory than with quietly exploring obscure corners of the globe, often alone, usually on the slenderest shoestring of a budget. In 1987 his progression from laser physicist, to school-teacher, to outdoor instructor, culminated in early retirement at the age of thirty-eight, with occasional instructing and guidebook writing bringing in enough cash to sustain life with his wife Jan in Snowdonia and long nomadic absences around the world.

Lindsay had been wanting for years to get to South Georgia and Julian was keen to invite him. I remembered the individuality that bordered on bloody-mindedness, the non-committal evasiveness, the inability to get up in the morning, the endless ritualistic cups of tea delaying departure, the slow pace, the antiquated equipment that always broke at crucial moments and all the other traits that had exasperated me in the past. Then I remembered that his wise re-siting of a dangerous camp on Shisha Pangma had probably saved four people from being wiped out by avalanches during the great storm. I had learned a lot from Lindsay and I reminded myself that, despite the occasional strain, our friendship had survived fourteen years and could quite well survive another three months on South Georgia. Lindsay could be exasperating but he was also one of the calmest, kindest people to have around, and we had spent some very enjoyable times together.

The fourth climber, Brian Davison, was another Tibet veteran. He grew up in County Durham, the son of a builder, started fell running in his teens, then took to 'the steeper bits', becoming a very competent rock climber while studying at Nottingham. There was something of the no-nonsense, plain-speaking, caricature northern scientist about him but he was also, like Lindsay, a bit of a loner, quiet, reclusive, and occasionally obtuse. He did not seem happy with the massed assault on Shisha Pangma, with its ramifications of team spirit and quasi-military camaraderie, and he did not perform particularly well at altitude. That at least was my impression, but Lindsay was keen that he should come to South Georgia.

In Tibet Brian's loyalties were divided between climbing the mountain and attempting to cooperate on under-resourced glaciological research. That difficult compromise must have accounted for his apparent fractiousness and poor performance on the mountain, for his record in Britain proved that he was a far more talented climber than any of us. He also, unlike us, had polar experience, having worked for the British Antarctic Survey. At twenty-nine he was now doing a PhD on background air sulphur levels, dividing his time between collecting samples in the Outer Hebrides and writing up results at Lancaster University. He was due for a break and, having already seen South Georgia on his way south in 1985, he was very keen to return and visit the island properly. On the principle that first impressions are usually wrong, I agreed to forget about Tibet and join the others in inviting Brian to join the team.

If Brian Davison was the token professional northerner, Kees 't Hooft, the Dutch film-maker, was our cosmopolitan man of the world, whose spiritual home is a cutting room in Soho with coffee and croissants, restaurants and good wine all to hand and the Opera just round the corner. I had met him whilst lodging with mutual friends in North London. Almost invariably his visits would be prefaced by the lilting Dutch voice announcing, 'I have brought a rather nice wine . . . it's a Barolo from Montanello,' or a rich dark 1983 Cahors, or some exquisitely indulgent Sauternes, carefully chilled and drunk with solemn ritual, to be followed, perhaps, by Dutch Sumatran cigars.

Kees, pronounced Case and short for Cornelius, was born in Delft in 1953. His father was a physics professor and his mother a musician. He was sent to the Montessori primary school and Lyceum and later studied film and photography at art college in Amsterdam, conforming briefly to the radical chic of the early Seventies. After prostituting himself to the advertising department of a chemical company he decided to return to the purity of film for art's sake and enrolled at the London International Film School. He has remained in London ever since, explaining flippantly that he lacks the ambition or efficiency to survive in Holland but can plod along quite contentedly in declining Britain. He also likes being a foreigner; even at the age of seven he had relished his differentness when he was sent to a French school in the Alps to recover from bronchitis. In France he also grew to love the mountains. In his twenties, when he came to London, he joined the celebrated North London Mountaineering Club but was dismayed by the climbing talent of most of its members. He admitted sadly that he was not a great natural climber. However, he became increasingly interested in climbers and why they climb, and his graduation project was a film portrait of a rock climber in North Wales.

Soon after I met Kees in 1987 I saw his five-minute rock climbing film. It was a shoestring production with no sound track, yet his camerawork and meticulous editing said far more about the sheer exuberance of climbing than many full length television documentaries. He still had virtually no professional experience as a cameraman, but had worked as assistant editor on major features including David Lean's *A Passage to India* and some outstanding documentaries such as Adrian Cowell's record of Amazonian deforestation, *The Decade of Destruction*. On a small-scale expedition film, that editing experience and his sensitivity as an observer would probably be more valuable than the technical skills of a seasoned cameraman reliant on a supervising director and astronomical expenses. What is more, Kees liked mountains and, in spite of being such a fastidious cultured person, could even tolerate mountaineers.

Our mutual friend Victor Saunders had already booked Kees to film in Nepal during the autumn of 1989, but I asked whether he could bear to follow three months in the Himalayas with another three months' discomfort on a sub-Antarctic island. I tempted him with visions of the sea voyage, the industrial archaeology of the whaling stations, the seals and penguins, and the wild mountain scenery, all just waiting to be filmed.

In June I took him up to Shropshire to meet Julian. It was a beautiful weekend and Kees, like everyone else, was seduced by it all: the roses cascading down the front of the cottage, the walk over the fields to see the new planting scheme in the family shrubbery, the swim in a meandering river on the Welsh border and the cave at Nescliff, whence one of Julian's more eccentric ancestors used to ambush stage coaches on the Holyhead Road. But he was most impressed by the fact this was not just some quasi-rural weekend retreat. Julian actually lived and belonged here and, as a planter of trees, was doing something genuinely valuable. As usual Julian talked a good deal of conservation and the environment. On his home ground he spoke with authority, but Kees already seemed a little wary of Julian's mission to extend his environmental concern and make the South Georgia expedition a statement about Antarctic conservation. He had commissioned an artist friend in Oswestry to paint a silver outline of Antarctica on green silk, with the words: *Southern Ocean Mountaineering Expedition supports Antarctica as a World Park.* It was a beautiful flag and we all agreed on the need to preserve the Antarctic wilderness; but some of us, nevertheless, were a little uneasy about banner-waving, all too aware that we had little expert knowledge of the complex issues involved. Only Brian had scientific experience in Antarctica, and that was in a fairly esoteric branch of glaciology. We wanted to see South Georgia and, on the basis that a journey needs some ostensible purpose, we were going there to climb mountains.

Kees disappeared to Nepal, promising that he would be back in time for the South Georgia trip. While he was away we made the final arrangements, booking flights to the Falklands, finding more sponsorship money, assembling equipment and, one afternoon, walking out of the supermarket with fifteen trolleys full of food to be packed in sealed plastic barrels for the voyage south. If everything went according to plan, half our supplies would be airlifted from the *Endurance*'s helicopter deck and dumped at Royal Bay, 25 miles south of the base at King Edward Point. We had stretched our luck asking Stormy Norm this extra favour, but he had said he would give it a try if he had time. With that depot in place it would be practical to attempt some of the unclimbed peaks right down at the southern end of the island.

Over the summer Julian and I had been piecing together the brief history of exploration and climbing on the island. In October we visited General Patrick Fagan, now head of military survey, who had been on a very successful expedition in 1965–6, repeating Shackleton's historic crossing, making first ascents of several peaks including the island's highest, Mt Paget, and doing a detailed survey of Royal Bay. He provided maps, invaluable advice and the enthusiasm of someone who had spent time on South Georgia and absorbed some of the island's special magic. But the real expert, the man who masterminded the whole survey of the island's interior during the Fifties, was Duncan Carse.

If I had been born a few years earlier I would probably remember the radio adventures of Dick Barton, Special Agent. The part was played by Duncan Carse, a well-known broadcaster who, like so many performers, was a recluse at heart. In the southern autumn of 1961 he bought for a shilling a lease of land on the deserted south-west coast of South Georgia and built a small hut there, hoping to remain entirely alone for eighteen months 'to achieve perspective in his personal relationship with an incomprehensible world'. One night, after three months, Carse was fast asleep when his hut was smashed to pieces by a freak wave, leaving him only the bare essentials for survival. He spent the next 116 winter days in a small tent before he was able to signal a passing sealing vessel which ferried him back to King Edward Point.

The Polar Record for that year recorded: '[Carse] says that he must repeat the experiment "without the tidal wave".' Although Carse did return again to South Georgia, the solo experiment was not repeated and his outstanding achievement remains the earlier expeditions of the 1950s. Four summers running he made his way south with different teams of mountaineers and surveyors to unravel the mysteries of the island's mountainous interior. There was probably no one else alive who knew the island so intimately, so it seemed a good idea for Julian and me to meet him.

When Julian first telephoned Carse the reaction was a little prickly but later, when we sent him our carefully written prospectus, he realised that we were not complete idiots and phoned back three times in one day to offer all kinds of useful advice. On November 1st we had to deliver our supplies to the *Endurance* at Portsmouth, so we asked if we could call in at Carse's Sussex home on the way back.

Julian stayed the night with me in Bath and at dawn we set off in his pick-up and trailer, loaded with thirty-three numbered, labelled barrels and a large bundle of skis and marker wands. At a service station on the motorway we met Kees, who had just returned from Nepal and wanted to film the loading of HMS *Endurance*. Never the most coordinated of people, he had fallen off the path leaving base camp and had had to hobble for two weeks back to Kathmandu on a sprained ankle; but he seemed quite unperturbed and confident that after a month's rest he would be ready for South Georgia.

The small red hull of the *Endurance* – known affectionately as the 'Plum' – looked incongruous, moored alongside towering grey frigates and aircraft carriers, and it was hard to believe that over 130 men would be living on the ship for the seven months' tour of duty. Trucks were lined up on the quay, loading provisions and apparently endless crates of beer on to conveyor belts and cranes. Our barrels were swung up in a net and lowered into the forward hold; then we were taken on board by the captain's secretary and given lunch in the wood-panelled wardroom. At this stage we didn't meet Captain Hodgson, but the first lieutenant, Nigel Davies, and the rest of the officers gave us a warm welcome.

We left Portsmouth after lunch and drove east to Sussex to meet Duncan Carse. Once again we were well entertained, with tea and cakes laid on by the explorer's gentle wife while Carse himself, white-haired, distinguished, courteous, directed operations in the resonant diction of a vanished age when broadcasters knew how to speak. He was interested in our film project and mentioned his own work with the BBC, but it was really South Georgia, his island, that he wanted to talk about. We did not have long so he rattled through some of the fine slides he had taken on his Leica thirty years earlier, pointing out mountains, glaciers and rocky headlands that he remembered in perfect detail.

The highest unclimbed peak on the island was named Mt Carse in his honour, and as it was our main objective he showed us distant shots of the mountain and of the route he had taken past it in 1955. 'Now this is the ridge you have to cross to get on to the Spenceley Glacier. Don't be tempted to go round it – you'll get into a horrible maze of crevasses. Much better to cross this little pass here. There's a good campsite just below it. Don't ask me why, but I camped there three times and always had good conditions. Now, here's the Spenceley, with Point 6854 up there in the top left corner and you can just see the tip of Carse right at the back . . . ' And so it continued, interspersed with anecdotes about the island's fickle weather, the fearsome katabatic winds, the sudden blizzards, the depots buried and lost under snow drifts . . . and the rare days of sunshine when the mountains gleamed, the sea was brilliant turquoise and the albatrosses danced in a crystal blue sky. 'You will love South Georgia and you'll want to go back.' He had hoped to return recently to climb his own mountain, 'but then I got this heart trouble. Damn nuisance, but it would have been too risky – an old man with a dicky heart. Anyway, if you get up it, make sure you send me a postcard.'

I could happily have stayed all evening but we still had one more engagement that day, at the Royal Geographical Society in London. A month before departure we still had no financial backing for Kees's film. I had been invited to a reception for film and television people at the RGS that evening and there was just a chance that we might interest someone in South Georgia. So we thanked the Carses, drove north and fought our way through the traffic to reach South Kensington just as the RGS party was coming to an end.

The whole of the exploring fraternity seemed to be there, along with a bevvy of cameramen, producers, directors and assorted groupies. Nearly everyone was drunk, coherent conversation was virtually impossible and, as far as we could see, everyone else was looking for money. Then I found Matt Dickinson, a young producer from a leading adventure film company, John Gau Productions. He was completely sober and prepared to listen while I told him that South Georgia was the most fascinating place on the globe and that Kees 't Hooft was an exciting new talent not to be missed. The mild-mannered Dutchman was called over and interrogated and the next day we had a phone call to say that Matt was very interested.

After a series of meetings, including one with John Gau himself, we had a speculative contract providing for the loan of £15,000-worth of Aaton 16 mm camera, sound recording equipment, a supply of film stock and the promise that the expedition's large deficit would be paid off afterwards if Kees's footage was suitable for a 25-minute slot on Central Television's *Voyager* adventure film series.

Five weeks after meeting Matt at the Royal Geographical Society we left for South Georgia.

3

South with the Plum

Sunday December 3rd, 1989 was a cold grey day. Rosie had flu and I did not feel much better. Nevertheless we spent the morning in the garden, planting 140 tulip bulbs, hoping that they might be coming to life when I returned from South Georgia in the spring. The strip of garden and small terrace house on the outskirts of Bath had been ours for only three months. It was my first proper home and I did not want to leave so soon.

On Monday evening Rosie drove me to RAF Brize Norton. On the way we stopped at a pub in the Cotswolds for a last quiet hour together, but after five minutes the familiar green pick-up parked outside and in walked Julian, Elaine, Kees and Lindsay. Julian had on the usual tweed outfit with a brand new wide-brimmed trilby, and was in an advanced state of manic excitement. Lindsay was characteristically quieter. He was looking forward to the trip but admitted that saying goodbye to Jan that morning had been hard. Elaine looked apprehensive and told Rosie she had taken the precaution of wearing waterproof mascara.

At the airport we were checked in by security guards with fixed bayonets. We found Brian in the departure lounge, where everything was ugly – the neon lights, the plastic seats, the machine dispensing foul coffee, the officious baggage handlers, the bored soldiers and the third-rate David Niven movie on the video screen. As soon as we had checked in our baggage, I went out to the car park to kiss Rosie goodbye. She drove away into the black night and I returned inside to join the four men who would be my inescapable companions for the next three and a half months.

Next day a sheep blocked the runway at Ascension Island and our plane had to circle over the sea for twenty minutes before it was safe to land. Then we skimmed down over low sea cliffs and fields of red and black lava, and dropped on to the now sheepless runway between hills bristling with satellite dishes. The island is administered by the Royal Air Force and was a crucial staging post in the 8000-mile journey of the 1982 Falklands Task Force. Wideawake Airbase is also shared by the US Air Force and NASA, which can use the phenomenally long runway as an emergency landing for the space shuttle. Security is paranoid and while the plane refuelled all the passengers, military and civilian, were herded into a wire cage where the squaddies had just one hour to drink as much beer as they could before the next nine-hour bout of strictly dry flying with the RAF.

Lindsay sipped orange juice, gazed up at the island's mountain and wished that he could stay a day and add it to his global repertoire of esoteric summits. The top of the volcano has its own micro-climate, with just enough moisture to support a lush crown of forest, much of it planted by early seafarers who came to this isolated speck of land near the equator to recuperate and repair ships ravaged by Atlantic storms. The coast, though, is an arid desert of cinders, and it was at one of the barren beaches here that sailors with contagious diseases were conveniently dumped and left to die.

After our brief equatorial respite we took off again for the next 4000 miles of Atlantic Ocean – hour after hour of blue sea, flecked white by the trade winds. Then we entered the zone of southern westerlies and the sea disappeared until we descended below clouds and flew in over the low fens and beaches of the Falklands archipelago.

On arrival at RAF Mount Pleasant all passengers are given a pep talk on the dangers of unexploded bombs and mines left by the Argentinians in 1982. An officer delivered his much-rehearsed speech, with an assistant holding up choice exhibits so that we should all know what to avoid stepping on. One particularly vicious anti-personnel mine had thin prongs of metal designed to explode into the victim's lower leg, maiming but not killing him. A dead comrade can be left, but a live wounded comrade, immobilised and writhing in agony, has to be looked after, diverting further manpower from the battle.

Major Tony Bleakley, the liaison officer responsible for military relations with the Falklands civilian population, had been detailed to look after the Southern Ocean Mountaineering Expedition, or SOMEX as we had been code-named. He was waiting with a Land-Rover to drive us to our quarters at the far end of the military complex, a mini-city rising incongruously out of the empty moorland. Lorries and Land-Rovers plied back and forth along the grid of tarmac roads in a scene of perpetual motion reminiscent of *MASH*. But the newness of the buildings, the vastness of the aircraft hangar and the high-tec defence installations added a modern touch of science fiction.

The accommodation quarters boast the world's longest corridor and it took us a good fifteen minutes to walk from our rooms up Tumbledown Lane to the Officers' Mess. Julian, Kees and I had come equipped with jackets and ties. Loan ties were found for the other two, but Lindsay insisted on appearing at the bar in his fluorescent fibre-pile jacket, swaying like some pink giraffe above a subdued herd of blazer and tweed. In fact the whole SOMEX entourage looked menacingly anarchic and it was a measure of the tolerance of the military staff that they were so hospitable during our five days in the Falklands.

During our stay we got some measure of the size of the operation to defend the islands. When the British government decided to build the new Mount Pleasant base, 30 miles from Port Stanley, a small town had to be built from scratch. All the construction materials, vehicles and military equipment had to be shipped 8000 miles from Britain and as long as the base exists it has to be resupplied continually. Fuel, food, equipment and gallons of duty-free alcohol have to be shipped 8000 miles down the Atlantic to the new harbour at East Cove. Fresh food, newspapers and mail are delivered with the twice weekly jet flights. Hundreds of men have to be entertained with bars, films, library and a huge sports hall. And all this, as they explained, is to keep a few jet fighter planes in the air. The whole strategy depends on air power and the supporting role of the army is to defend the airfield.

One day we flew in a helicopter to see some of the sites of the 1982 conflict. Goose Green had only the sketchiest undulations and scraggy gorse bushes for cover. Further west, on the far shore of Falkland Sound, our guide pointed out the shallow valley, running parallel to the shore and protected by a low ridge, which enabled Argentinian jets to skim the ground, invisible to radar until the last moment when they banked sharply to the right and screamed across the Sound into San Carlos Water to bombard the vulnerable British ships. On the shore, near the red tin-roofed houses of San Carlos settlement, the Union Jack flew over a circular cemetery; but it was only when we saw the main war memorial in Port Stanley that I appreciated just how many men had died retaking the islands.

We were there at midsummer. The sun shone out of wide blue skies and the hills had a luminous clarity unimaginable in Europe, confusing one's normal perceptions of scale and distance. Port Stanley seemed exotic, with its red and green painted roofs overlooking the harbour. In reality, it is a tiny provincial town, servicing the far flung communities of 'the camp' – the isolated sheep farming settlements, most of which have no road. When we had lunch at the Malvina restaurant and asked if we could take a photo the landlord replied conspiratorially, 'Well, hold on a moment and I'll just check that there's no one here having lunch with someone else's wife.' Apparently adultery is rife and the police station has some morbid photographic exhibits of past *crimes passionnels*.

One evening Julian and I gave a lecture on the Himalaya at the school in Port Stanley. I had prepared a special shortened version of my Everest slideshow, removing all slides peripheral to the main story and keeping just the most dramatic action pictures. Unfortunately I discovered at the last moment that I had brought the reject slides and left the crucial set 8000 miles away in Bath. While Julian chatted with the schoolteacher I went very, very quiet and pondered suicide. In the end, after a drink at the pub to relieve my dry mouth, I did my best to entertain our audience, cobbling together a brief slide introduction with the few pictures I had, then switching off the projector and resorting to some inspired drawing on the blackboard. The audience clearly had the imaginative power (or was it just politeness?) to rise to the occasion and they seemed to enjoy the evening, forgiving my blunder and giving both of us a warm welcome.

The following day a girl soldier drove us along the 30-mile gravel road back to Mount Pleasant. After a lunchtime drinking session at the Upland Goose I had inevitably to ask her to stop the vehicle before we reached base. As I clambered out of the back of the Land-Rover and headed into the nearest minefield, she gave a look of withering despair at her unmanly civilian passengers. Back at Mount Pleasant she announced, 'It says on my sheet that I'm supposed to be taking you to scrum with Biffy.'

'Scrum with Biffy?'

She looked even more despairing. 'Scrum – you know – dinner.'

'Ah! But who's Biffy?'

'C. Biffy. The boss. You know – General Stevenson – CBFFI – Commander of British Forces in the Falkland Islands.'

This was the first we had heard of a dinner invitation, but the corporal showed us the schedule where it was clearly written that we were to dine with CBFFI that evening before lecturing in the Joint Education Centre. We thought there might be a mistake but dared not offend the general, so we hurriedly washed and tried to make our one set of smart clothes look cleaner. Kees and I looked vaguely sartorial. Julian's crumpled tweeds were redolent not so much of the grouse moor as a spot of rabbit poaching. Brian seemed to have lost the loan tie and Lindsay still had on the patched climbing trousers and pink jacket. At 7 p.m. we walked up to the Commander's house, a suburban brick job reminiscent of Milton Keynes, rising incongruously from the windswept moorland of East Falkland.

One glance through the window was enough to reveal two men and two women sitting down to dinner at a table laid for four. But by now we had rung the bell and there was no turning back. A uniformed ADC opened the door, glanced nervously up at the pink giraffe, then stared in horror at the rest of us. 'They've just sat down to dinner.'

'So we're not expected?'

'No. It's just the General and Mrs Stevenson, CIBFAI and his wife. I think they're coming to your lecture and having you here for drinks afterwards.'

'Sorry, there's been a mistake. Don't worry, we'll go away.'

CIBFAI proved to be the Commander of British Forces on

Ascension Island, on official visit to the Falklands. Along with the rest of the dinner party, he dutifully turned up to our lecture to swell a small but enthusiastic audience. This time I had the full panoply of military teaching aids and followed my few slides with some elaborate coloured diagrams on the demonstration board. Afterwards Mrs Biffy said that she enjoyed the bit without slides best, which made me wonder whether I shouldn't forget about photography and stick in future to lecturing with just a picture board.

Paul Stevenson apologised for the mix-up over dinner and invited us back for drinks. It was nice at last to meet the man who had full responsibility for all the land, sea and air forces in the South Atlantic and had been prepared to take the risk of authorising our expedition. We chatted about mutual iconoclastic acquaintances in the Royal Marines, Julian extolled the virtues of tree-planting to Mrs Biffy, Brian told stories of his days with the British Antarctic Survey, the drink flowed, Kees produced the Sumatran cigars and CIBFAI invited us all to stay at Ascension Island on the way home.

After that excellent evening with the military boss we were driven back to Port Stanley on our last day, for lunch with the civilian establishment at Government House. It reminded me of one of those rambling, gabled, seaside houses in Devon or Corn-wall, with wind-blasted gorse hedges around the garden, luxuriant banks of petunias and a huge vine in the conservatory, and a large chintzy sitting-room redolent of old world comfort. However, there were ambassadorial touches such as the Union Jack and the Governor's car, an old maroon London taxi with the royal crest by way of a number plate. His Excellency, W. H. Fullerton and his wife were both enthusiastic about their job and the conversation around the dining table centred on the South Atlantic. The previous summer they had visited South Georgia and the Antarctic Peninsula with HMS *Endurance*, which is seen very much as 'the Governor's ship'; but most of their time is taken up with the day-to-day administration of the Falklands.

Perhaps the most important development since 1982 has been the establishment of a commercial fisheries board with jurisdiction over all the waters within a 150-mile radius of Port Stanley.

Licences bring in revenue and are a means of conserving squid stocks but, as Mr Fullerton pointed out, there are problems. Policing the fishing zone eats up a large proportion of the revenue and not all the squid stay conveniently within the zone. 'We can keep quite a tight control on one squid species but there are others which range much further out. So these big trawling fleets can sit just outside the 150-mile zone, hauling in huge catches, and there is nothing we can do about it.'

The immediate problems of the Falklands fishing grounds led on to Antarctic conservation in general. Julian plunged in head first with the fiery zeal of the amateur conservationist, to be refuted at almost every turn by Nigel Bonner, a biologist who had been working on South Georgia before most of us were born. Julian was of course utterly sincere, but Bonner spoke with the dispassionate authority of a scientist. He looked the part, with a patriarchal white beard worthy of Darwin, and if his objectivity about fishing, sealing and whaling bordered on the callous, it was at least based on real experience. Back in the sitting-room for coffee, Mrs Fullerton steered the conversation to less emotive topics, but Julian was to have further opportunities for parrying with Bonner as he too was embarking the next day on HMS *Endurance* for the crossing to South Georgia.

Nothing could have been further from the midnight horrors of Brize Norton six days earlier. We sailed from East Cove on a radiant afternoon, the Plum glowing red against a calm blue sea, with only the gentlest roll and the comforting vibration of the engine to show that we were moving. Kees, Brian and Lindsay had sleeping quarters in the airless, lightless library, far below deck, but as one of the SOMEX 'leaders' I was lucky enough to have a cabin shared with Gavin Drabble, the captain's secretary, Ian Abson, one of the helicopter flight observers, and a rather shy young Uruguayan naval officer who had joined the ship in Montevideo.

Gavin asked me politely to keep my stuff tidy as space was very tight and the tiny cabin was their only home for seven months. Discipline and tidiness seemed to be paramount throughout the ship, with clearly defined limits of space keeping anarchy at bay.

At dinner the officers wore cummerbunds over spotless white shirts and we were asked to wear jackets and ties. As we assembled in the panelled wardroom to meet all the other guests, wondering who they all were, I couldn't help thinking of similar gatherings in Agatha Christie stories. It would have made a good setting for a murder, but the only potential for discord was Julian's discovery that most of our fellow-passengers had some connection with the defunct whaling industry.

Ian Hart was researching a book on the original Compañía Argentina de Pesca. Lyle Craigie-Halkett and Roy Martin had been sent out by the present owner of all the abandoned whaling stations, Christian Salvesen, to assess the salvage potential; Nigel Bonner was doing an independent survey for the Foreign and Commonwealth Office. Phil Rotier from the Scott Polar Research Institute planned to make acoustic recordings of background noise in Cumberland Bay for possible use by the Admiralty. And there was Rolf, a gigantic Scandinavian, eighty years old, who had worked as a whaler on South Georgia in younger days. All those carcasses had left him a committed carnivore, devouring platefuls of meat at every meal and grunting between mouthfuls, 'I never touch vegetables.'

As soon as the guests had finished dinner we had to make way for the officers, who had been waiting patiently at the bar. I cannot remember all their names but Fred, the engineer, and Malcolm Nelms, the meteorology officer, were the most jovial, while the Scottish ship's doctor delivered a wry commentary on life in the South Atlantic. Nigel Davies, the first lieutenant, was very friendly and impeccably polite, always preceding any request with 'Gentlemen, would you mind . . . ' and of all the officers he was perhaps the most enthusiastic about our project, having been on a services expedition to Elephant Island.

After dinner Kees and I visited the bridge where John Saunders, chief navigator and head of operations, was on duty. He was quietly spoken and sartorial in his crimson cummerbund. I tried to follow his explanation of the navigation systems as he twiddled a few knobs on the satellite computer and discovered in seconds the ship's distance, accurate to a few yards, from his wife and children near Portsmouth. Talk of navigation got him on to 1982 when he had sailed south in HMS *Antrim*, stopping at Ascension Island to borrow the new Magnavox satellite navigation equipment from the *Sheffield*. The *Antrim* was part of the highly secret Operation Paraquat, separate from the main task force and destined for South Georgia. On board were some of the Royal Marines, SAS and SBS (Special Boat Squadron) soldiers sent to retake the island. Once King Edward Point was secure the *Antrim* then sailed back west to the Falklands, where her hull was pierced by an Argentinian bomb which lodged itself, unexploded, in the aft heads.

Eight thousand miles away in London, the Admiralty advised against trying to move it. But the men on the *Antrim* were not happy about a large unexploded bomb sitting in the ship's lavatories so they manhandled it very carefully out into the sea. John Saunders told the story with the guilty, proud smile of a schoolboy playing with home-made explosives, but admitted that at the time it had been very, very frightening.

Monday December 11th was another perfect day. I was woken from a deep sleep by the shrill tootling of the bosun's whistle, then became slowly aware of the gentle rocking motion, the slurping and gurgling of water against the ship, and the movements of my cabin mates going on watch. Soon I climbed down from my bunk and went into the adjoining shower room to look out of the porthole at sun, sky and marbled turquoise water frothing past the red hull. The birds were still with us, wheeling, skimming and diving in effortless rhythm – the ugly yellow-eyed giant petrels, little piebald Cape pigeons, the black browed albatross, like a large version of our black-backed gull, and the much bigger, whiter wandering albatross. Later that summer French scientists published the results of tracking a wandering albatross by satellite. In thirty-three days it flew 10,000 miles, averaging 303 miles a day but sometimes covering as much as 600 miles, often managing on just one hour's sleep a day.

Our first full day aboard passed in idle enjoyment. On deck there was the constant sun and breeze and the delightful sensation of being surrounded by vast tracts of empty ocean, but we spent the afternoon in the wardroom, watching the video of a documentary on South Georgia by Duncan Carse. Then we had more vicarious adventure, with Chris Ralling's dramatised documentary on the life of Shackleton. There was a nice sense of a continuing tradition, with Shackleton's portrait hanging on the wall, his famous square jaw dominating the room. Even the ship's boats on the modern *Endurance* are named after Shackleton's. There is a rigid inflatable called the *Dudley Docker* and, hanging in davits on the foredeck, two motor launches, the *Stanscombe Wills*, and the hydrographic survey boat, the *James Caird*. Because Shackleton failed to set foot on the Antarctic continent in 1914 he was unable to name new territory after his principal sponsors and they had to make do with lifeboats, but their names are now immortalised by the Royal Navy.

The mother ship was originally called *Anita Dan* and was used for carrying passengers and freight between Iceland, Greenland and Spitzbergen. In 1968 the Royal Navy bought her from the Danes for her scrap value of £300,000, and spent £2 million on refitting before relaunching her as HMS *Endurance*. One of the things that remained unchanged was the old Burmeister & Wains 5-cylinder diesel engine. It is slow, with a maximum speed of 13½ knots, but, given loving care and attention, reliable. Having never seen anything bigger than a standard car engine I was impressed, on the second day of our passage, when we put on overalls and ear protectors and went down into the bowels of the ship to see the engine room. The main engine, with its 9-inch valve springs banging relentlessly up and down, guzzling 7½ tons of fuel a day, seemed massive, but by modern standards it is apparently small. Shouting explanations above the din, the engineer showed us all the ancillary equipment – the banks of electronic controls, the generator motor, the desalination plants, back-up pump motors and a 15-foot-square sewage treatment tank, just installed to comply with new regulations in Antarctic waters.

Then we went aft through a hydraulic steel fire door into a long narrow tunnel containing the single prop shaft, whizzing round in its housings. This archaic system, with just a single spinning screw and no gearing, makes the *Endurance* a notoriously difficult ship to 'drive'. Nowadays a captain usually has twin screws, and per-haps stern and bow thrusters, to steer with, but on the *Endurance* he has just the rudder and the one propeller. If he needs suddenly to go backwards the engine has to be stopped completely before it can be put into reverse. This lack of manoeuvrability can make for some fraught sailing in the Antarctic pack ice, especially as the ship was designed for only occasional brushes with ice in the Danish sub-Arctic. The sharply sloping bow, strengthened with one-inch plate, can cope to a point but she is not a proper ice-breaker and the previous year, during the Governor's southern tour, one obstinate iceberg had gashed a large hole in the hull, just missing the engine room bulkhead.

The ship's helicopters are often used to reconnoitre leads in the ice and the captain can also position someone forward of the bridge in a special lookout tower. At this stage, of course, we were still well north of any pack ice. Captain Hodgson was in an affable mood and seemed pro-SOMEX. The five of us had performed on the ship's video 'news' and the captain had attended our little lecture in the junior ranks dining-room, when Julian outlined what we hoped to achieve on South Georgia and I repeated the now highly polished Everest blackboard routine.

Now, on Tuesday morning, he let me come up on to the bridge and take some pictures. He was in a particularly good mood because a junior rating had just appeared with a vital spare heli-copter part that had been missing since the ship sailed from Portsmouth. Malcolm Nelms, who was on watch at the time, beamed serenely at his contented boss while the captain himself enthused about his new command: 'I'm a submariner by trade but I love this job. I love this ship, even though she's thirty years old and a lot of the parts were made twenty years before that so it's impossible to get replacements . . . but she's a wonderful ship, I'm my own boss and the Admiralty's 8000 miles away.'

He continued in the same genial vein, hoping that perhaps, now that relations with Argentina were improving rapidly, his su-periors might even ask him to take the *Endurance* to Buenos Aires as part of a goodwill mission. It seemed a good idea to me. After all, the ship's main function is scientific. She has her detachment of twelve Royal Marines and the Lynx helicopters can be fitted with effective missiles, but her only visible weaponry is the pair of ancient 20 mm Oerlikons. So I turned to this senior captain in the Royal Navy, renowned for his short temper, and said casually,

'Yes, I suppose it would be suitable because you could hardly call her a warship.'

Malcolm looked panic stricken. The Captain made a funny face and laughed uneasily and, as I back-pedalled frantically, all confused and red in the face, he warned, 'Watch it, sonny. That's not the way to go about getting your helicopter drop in Royal Bay.'

My gaffe must have been forgiven for the following night Julian and I were invited to dinner with the Captain. In fact, the closest contact the *Endurance* made with Argentina later that season was a friendly football match at one of the Argentinian scientific bases on the Antarctic Peninsula. But even that modest gesture of friendship caused a storm of protest from the Falklanders, whose cries of 'Betrayal' made good fodder for the British press. It might seem ridiculous to get that angry about a football match, but in Port Stanley the headteacher who organised our talk had shown us the strength of outrage felt by most Falklanders: 'After what they did to us, we don't ever want the Argentinians back. I might consider any country ruling us . . . but not Argentina.'

Later that morning we did some filming on the forecastle. Kees was growing ever fonder of the Aaton 16 mm camera but always needed an assistant to handle the Dog – a high performance microphone encased in a sleeve of shaggy fur to dampen wind noise. So we took it in turns to wear headphones, adjust levels on the professional Walkman and point the Dog at the current victim of Kees's investigative eye.

Today it was interview time and each of us had to speak a small piece about what had brought us sailing south with HMS *Endurance*. I tried the nostalgic line, recalling my reading of Shackleton twenty years earlier. Brian looked embarrassed and mumbled something about his work with the British Antarctic Survey. Julian delivered a statement from the despatch box. Lindsay, looking like some weather-beaten old hippy, started off in his most casual chatty tones, 'Well . . . a few years ago I was leafing through this French magazine . . . ' – he paused for the audience to summon up images of much-fingered pornography – 'when I suddenly came across some photos . . . of these amazing mountains!'

We were now only about 250 miles from those mountains. The

previous night we had crossed the Antarctic Convergence and today there was some fog and a definite bite to the air. There is no temperate zone in the Southern Ocean, just this sudden change from warm to cold. If anyone was to fall overboard here he would probably freeze to death in minutes. While we were doing the fourth retake of 'leafing through this French magazine', Brian suddenly shouted 'Look!' and there, just over the side, was our first seal, flipping its playful arch through the waves. That evening we saw the distant grey oblong of an iceberg and as we sat on the upper deck with our after-dinner cigars, it was exciting to think that when we awoke the next morning we would see South Georgia.

What we actually saw was a lot of cloud and drizzle and a dawn so darkly subtle that it almost passed unnoticed. Nevertheless Julian was up at first light, manically striding the decks and declaring 'Sound country!' when we finally glimpsed some sodden black cliffs slinking past in the murk.

Kees was filming everything, undeterred by the drizzle, and as we steamed into Stromness Bay I had the Dog primed to record a sudden cacophony of activity. The *Dudley Docker* was lowered into the water and roared off towards the old whaling station at Husvik, starting a long day of ferrying people, mail and supplies ashore. Then Kees and I rushed aft to the helicopter hangar to record the action there. Once again I was impressed by the meticulous professionalism of officers and crew. Engineers had been up late the previous night checking and rechecking every minute part and now there was the most elaborate procedure for wheeling the first Lynx out on to the flight deck, lashing it firmly down, opening the folding rotor blades, fuelling and carrying out final checks. Once the pilot and navigator were aboard with engines running, the four support crew removed the securing straps, walked back to the hangar and stood in a line, holding up the straps to show that the aircraft was free, while Malcolm, looking rather un-naval in a woolly pom-pom hat and ear protectors, waved his arms in an elaborate set of signals for lift-off.

The *Endurance* was not due at King Edward Point until Thursday and all Wednesday she remained at anchor in Stromness Bay, with the Union Jack flying from the forecastle. After a dismal dawn the weather improved enough for the helicopter crews to carry out some of their planned aerial survey programme, part of the Admiralty's continuing hydrographic survey to improve the accuracy of charts. As my cabin mate, Ian Abson, explained, 'The topography is very accurate, but they still haven't got South Georgia pointing in quite the right direction.' He reappeared in the bar at lunchtime and gulped down three pints of lemonade to put back some of the liquid lost during a morning of sweltering work in regulation warm clothing and rubberised survival suit. Flying helicopters in South Georgia is notoriously dangerous and the crews have to be equipped at all times to survive being stranded on a glacier or ditched in the frigid sea.

That afternoon the clouds lifted briefly to reveal a glimpse of icy summits behind the lower hills encircling Stromness Bay. Most of the time the interior remained hidden but the weather improved in the bay and by evening the rusty oil tanks and factory buildings at Husvik, three miles away, were glowing russet in the sunlight. The grey beaches and mossy slopes above were littered with brown blobs of seal and thousands of tiny pale sticks, indicating penguins. To the west of Husvik I could see the hills Shackleton, Worsley and Crean had crossed on the final leg of their desperate rescue mission. Behind us sedimentary cliffs were wrenched and twisted by primeval forces into the distinctive streaks which Shackleton had recognised when he first looked down into Stromness Bay:

> The twisted, wave-like rock-formations of Husvik Harbour appeared right ahead in the opening of dawn. Without a word we shook hands with one another. To our minds the journey was over, though as a matter of fact twelve miles of difficult country had still to be traversed.

We had reached this place with minimal effort as the pampered guests of the Royal Navy; even so, seeing the country for myself, I was beginning to warm to the special magic of this wilderness with its superimposed aura of human legend.

Captain Hodgson was also, after an apparently fraught day on the bridge, mellowing to the romance of the South. Julian and I could not have asked for a more genial host when we joined him for supper in his small sitting-room.

While we dined on the top deck Kees, unfettered by English hierarchic inhibitions, joined the junior ranks below for their weekly beer and bingo session. Later we were all back in the wardroom, celebrating our last night on board with cigars and malt whisky. The mellowing process continued unchecked until midnight when the flight commander suddenly announced that our Royal Bay helicopter depot was to go ahead the next morning. So the five of us had to stagger woolly-headed into the bowels of the ship, manoeuvring Lindsay through narrow companionways to the forward hold, where we thrashed around in a tangle of netting to sort out our baggage, separating the eighteen barrels labelled 'RB' to haul, slide and roll them laboriously back to the helicopter hangar at the far end of the ship.

When I sat down to breakfast the next day we were already steaming round the headland to the next great indentation in South Georgia's north-east coast, Cumberland Bay. Once again it was a day of intense activity. The helicopter took off with half our barrels in a net, returned fifteen minutes later for the second load, then transported a detachment of Royal Engineers to carry out a land survey on the far side of Royal Bay. Meanwhile the ship was swinging in a wide arc past Cumberland West Bay and into the East Bay, with Nigel Davies and John Saunders dashing repeatedly in and out of the bridge to squint through side-mounted compasses and check bearings off the jagged crenellations of the shore.

The wind came suddenly, in a cold blast from the glaciers, whipping spume off the sea and juddering the ship. It was our first experience of the katabatic 'williewaws' that funnel down from the high mountains into the fjords of South Georgia's lee coast. Today the mountains were hidden and we could see only the tongues of their glaciers reaching down below the clouds. Deep in the cleft of Moraine Fjord, the Harker and Hamburg tumbled chaotically into the sea, but further left, the Nordenskjöld was a broad shelf floating at the head of the bay, its vertical front glowing pale blue.

The SOMEX team was now assembled on the starboard deck, fighting its way into survival suits and lifejackets. Brian had been here before, on his way south with BAS, and pointed out Shackleton's memorial cross on a grass headland. Then, as we glided past the headland, the rusty ghost town of Grytviken, a replica of Husvik, slid into view. It sits at the back of King Edward Cove, a perfect natural harbour in the arm of the mountains, hidden away from the ocean at right angles to Cumberland East Bay. Only at the last moment did we see the red, green and white huts of King Edward Point. There was a clattering roar of iron as hundreds of tons of anchor chain plunged into the sea, then the landing craft were lowered over the side. Lindsay, Brian and Julian went ashore with the remaining barrels in the bigger boat. Kees and I followed in the bucking *Dudley Docker*, bracing our knees to stay upright, while Kees filmed and I pointed the Dog with one hand and waved goodbye to the *Endurance* with the other.

Five minutes later the outboard motor was quiet and we climbed out on to the concrete jetty of King Edward Point, the most southerly outpost of the dwindling British Empire.

4

Antarctic Graveyard

'I'm afraid we've had to put you in the post office, as we're rather full up at the moment, but of course you can eat here.' Major Matt O'Hanlon, the Anglo-Irish commanding officer, hardly needed to apologise for expeditions were traditionally housed in less than luxury and during the Fifties all Duncan Carse's despatches to *The Times* had been headed, 'The Gaol, King Edward Point, Cumberland East Bay, South Georgia'. Matt was sorting out accommodation with Julian and the others when I arrived at the main accommodation building, called, inevitably, Shackleton House.

The mess was a friendly room panelled in yellowing pine. The bar top was gleaming copper and the electric lights were fitted inside old ships' lanterns. Almost every foot of wall space was hung with nautical and polar bric-a-brac: a pair of Canadian snowshoes framing a window, ships' bells and wheels, a globe, a helicopter blade, balalaikas donated by Russian trawlermen, sledging photos by Duncan Carse, sketchy old charts of the island, ships' pennants, whaling harpoons and a piece of whale baleen. There were official photos of the Queen, of C. Biffy and of King Edward VII, in whose reign the settlement was established. Captain Cook was also honoured and a whole corner was set aside for Shackleton, with 'a token of appreciation to Bro. Sir Ernest Shackleton CVO from the English masons of Uruguay Acacia Lodge No. 876' and a bronze plaque 'from His Britannic Majesty's chargé d'affaires on behalf of His Majesty's Government, Montevideo, February 1922'.

Shackleton died, ironically, at anchor off South Georgia, only six years after his extraordinary crossing of the island. He was setting out on what was intended to be the last great polar expedition, but ever since joining Scott's first Antarctic expedition in 1902 he had been troubled by a suspect heart. Now, aged only forty-seven, he died of a massive heart attack aboard the expedition ship, *Quest*. His colleagues sailed with Shackleton's body to Montevideo, but at his wife's request they returned to bury him on South Georgia.

In the mess there was also a set of King Edward Point photos, going back to the mid-Sixties, portraying the annual groups of British Antarctic Survey scientists who had administered the island during the Seventies. Then suddenly, after 1982, the haphazard groupings of long-haired, bearded scientists in standard-issue Norwegian jerseys gave way to rigid school photos of the new military detachments, jaw-jutting in impeccable straight lines. The photos were formal but the day-to-day life of the garrison seemed quite relaxed. Officers and NCOs – and there were only eight of them in all – shared the same mess and spent most of the time in civilian clothes. Matt, the commander, was only thirty-one and the two Royal Marine sergeants in charge of boats and mountain training were hardly older. As for the squaddies, many of them were teenagers from the Green Howard regiment, based at Catterick, and had barely ventured outside North Yorkshire before. It was slightly depressing for us mountaineers to realise that, apart from Brian, we were older than everyone in the garrison.

The army has inevitably stamped some of its personality on the settlement and some of the refinements have gone. In 1967, when Bill Tilman anchored his cutter, *Mischief*, in the Cove, he was entertained at the civilian Magistrate's house and recorded:

> Adjoining the living-room was a built-on conservatory where under Mrs Coleman's devoted care, geraniums, roses, fuchsias and other flowers flourished exceedingly. Nor can there be many, if any, other conservatories in the world whence you can look down upon families of sea elephants lying blissfully asleep in their mud wallows among tussock grass. Indeed, if you opened the conservatory windows you could smell them.

We met the seals for ourselves after lunch. We were settling into the post office, unpacking luggage on to the iron bedsteads that provided havens amongst piles of old files and ledgers, when Brian called, 'Come and look here!' Behind the building, sprawled in the grass, were a dozen seals with pale grey coats glistening in the sun.

I knelt down and combed my fingers through one of their sleek coats. 'Are they fur seals?'

'No, they'd be biting your legs if they were. No, these are young elephant pups, probably only a few weeks old.'

Already they were about five feet long and completely independent, with no sign of parents around. We spent about an hour entranced by the scene of soporific indolence. Occasionally, if one approached too close, a seal would lift its head and belch; but for the most part they remained flat on their backs, soaking up the hot sun and scratching themselves with the beautifully articulated claws of their front flippers. All the while, irritated by endemic nasal mites, they snorted with the gentle farting noise that I will always associate with South Georgia. They were very charming but later, near the graveyard, I met my first adult bull, wallowing his three or four tons of flesh, blubber and half-moulted fur in a foetid muddy pool. As I walked a little closer he reared up his chest seven feet high, opened a cavernous pink mouth and set his proboscis wobbling in a massive belch, blasting me with a steam cloud of halitosis. The bull's sheer bulk and prodigious snout were awesome – small wonder that the early explorers called the beasts 'sea elephants', a term now prosified to the official 'elephant seal'.

A gravel road leads round from the tiny peninsula of King Edward Point to Grytviken on the far side of the cove. Even on the finest afternoons there is usually enough breeze to set loose sheets of corrugated iron flapping. The mournful banging of old iron and the hiss of leaking water pipes are the only sounds in the ghost town. The only remaining ships are the rotting hulk of the *Louise*, which transported coal when the station was established in 1904, two sealing boats scuttled by vandals in 1980 and now lying askew in the water, and the *Petrel*, claimed to be the world's last floating whale catcher, moored at the rotting jetty as testament to a dead industry.

The *Petrel* is a typical Norwegian whale catcher – small, light and fast, with an elegant curve to the bow and a prominent lookout mast. Originally there would have been a gangplank linking the bridge to the harpoon gun platform on the bows, allowing the chief gunner, invariably a Scandinavian, to rush forward at the last moment, take aim and fire. The gangplank has gone but the gun remains, pointing defiantly at the sky. The harpoon shaft is nearly two metres of heavy steel, culminating in four massive barbs, which would spring open as the harpoon head exploded in the whale's flesh. At first the explosive heads were sharply pointed, but they sometimes shot right through the whale, so they were replaced by blunter heads guaranteed to explode with maximum effect in the whale's side. When the whaling stopped in 1965 many of these harpoon heads were unused and they still litter the ground at Grytviken.

Three months later, at the end of the expedition, Julian and I explored the inside of the *Petrel*, finding a companionway down into the hull leading to the crew's living quarters. The wooden bunks were tiny wedge-shaped coffins, stacked right up into the apex of the bows, around a cramped little dining-room. It must have been a miserable place to live, with the boat bucking in a Force Nine, but the officers' quarters at the stern were not much roomier for, as in a tug, maximum space had to be reserved for the powerful engines. It was a hard life but a summer's whaling season earned the men, mainly Scandinavians, enough money to support their families at home for the whole year. The industry became highly efficient and profitable and was the catalyst that transformed Norway from a poor nation of farmers and small-time fishermen into a major industrial power. Norway developed her own heavy engineering and a specialised shipbuilding industry; the harpoon technology was developed into more sophisticated explosives designed to destroy humans and Konsberg Vapenfabric became one of the world's leading armaments companies.

The industry on South Georgia was founded largely through the vision of one man, Captain Carl Anton Larsen. He first visited Antarctica in 1892, the same year that a Scottish expedition was also investigating the potential for whaling in southern waters. Larsen first saw South Georgia during his second voyage in 1894, and two years later he made enquiries to the Royal Geographical Society in London about the possibility of setting up a whaling station on the island.

One of the Lynxes lifts expedition supplies for the drop at Royal Bay, as HMS *Endurance* approaches the island.

Shackleton's cross at King Edward Point. HMS *Endurance* is anchored in Cumberland East Bay, with the Barff Peninsula and Sörling Valley behind.

Two fur seals enjoying the sun-warmed jetty at Leith Harbour - the abandoned whaling station where the Argentinians landed in 1982.

A small colony of gentoo penguins on the football pitch at Leith Harbour.

The flensing plan at Grytviken in the 1950s with several whale carcasses being processed. The buildings of King Edward Point are visible beyond the ship's stern. (*Photo by Duncan Carse*)

Grytviken today. The steam-powered bone saw and bone cooker hatches remain rusting on the upper deck.

Albatross and *Dias*, two derelict whalers, lie half sunk at the jetty amidst a pile of debris.

Crossing Cumberland East Bay in the *Stanscombe Wills*.
Left to right: Julian Freeman-Attwood, Kees 't Hooft, Brian Davison and Lindsay Griffin.

Brian with outraged elephant and fur seal pups on the beach at St Andrew's Bay.

A king penguin watches the author reload his camera at St Andrew's Bay.
(*Photo by Julian Freeman-Attwood*)

Typical South Georgia weather, with lenticular wave clouds pouring over the mountains onto the Nordenskjöld Glacier.

Detail of the Nordenskjöld Glacier with its two distinctive medial moraines of black rock. The cliff face is about 150 feet high.

Brian emerging from the front door of the snowcave. A frozen lake still fills the bottom of the windscoop.

The South Wing of the snowcave, with one of the tents pitched on the left.

Julian and Kees on a rare outing from the snowcave. To the north-west the evening sun illuminates (r to l) the rocky ribs of Nordenskjöld Peak, the snow pyramid of Mt Roots and the distant bulk of Mt Paget.

Julian and Lindsay on the first ascent of Mt Vogel. In the background the Spenceley Glacier slopes down to the west coast of the island.

Royal Bay. A pod of elephant seals in typical pose where the Ross Glacier tumbles into Little Moltke Harbour. Tiny Cape pigeons are fishing in the surf, which is blasted back out to sea by a violent offshore wind.

Angry skuas protect their nest on Cumberland East Bay.

Larsen sailed south again with the Swedish South Polar Expedition of 1901–3, led by Otto Nordenskjöld. Larsen was captain of the expedition ship, the *Antarctic*, and after disembarking Nordenskjöld's party for scientific work on the Antarctic Peninsula, he sailed back north to Tierra del Fuego, the Falklands and South Georgia, where he spent most of the Austral winter of 1902 surveying, geologising and botanising. At the end of the year he sailed south to relieve the land party.

Larsen was now embroiled in one of the great epics of Antarctic exploration. Like the *Endurance* twelve years later, the *Antarctic* was defeated by the Weddell Sea pack ice. Larsen managed to land one relief party at Hope Bay, opposite Nordenskjöld's party on Snow Hill, but they were unable to sledge across the intervening sea ice. Later Larsen and the rest of the crew were forced to abandon ship and sledge to the deserted Paulet Island when the *Antarctic* was crushed and sank. That left three separate parties marooned for another Antarctic winter, surviving mainly on penguin and seal meat. After months of unspeakable hardship and harrowing sledging journeys all three parties were finally reunited the following spring at Snow Hill, just as the Argentinian navy came to their rescue.

Larsen's name was immortalised in the Larsen Ice Shelf along the east coast of the Antarctic peninsula, but he was to make his real mark on South Georgia. He had seen the commercial potential of the island and at a banquet in Buenos Aires after the rescue from Snow Hill, he enthused about 'dems vary big vales and I see dem in houndred and tousends'. There was clearly money to be made, but in the past Larsen had failed to find backing in Norway, just as the Scotsman, W. S. Bruce, had failed after his 1892 voyage to interest his country. Now, at last, shareholders were found in Argentina. By Christmas 1904 Larsen had formed his Compañía Argentina de Pesca and the first whales were being processed at his new South Georgia shore station of Grytviken. In those days Cumberland Bay was teeming with humped-backed whales and the profusion of easy prey, close to shore, made for rapid profits. But as the industry expanded with further stations springing up in the island's other natural harbours, the whale catchers were forced to sail further out into the ocean.

In 1928, when a Dr Ludwig Kohl-Larsen and his wife visited the island on a private scientific expedition, they noted that already the hump-backed whales were very rare. None were taken that year and the catchers were having to travel further for the sperm, fin, sei and blue whales. Nevertheless, huge profits were still being made. The oil and by-products from a ninety-foot blue whale, for instance, made about £2,500. In 1912 the largest whale ever caught – 112 feet long and over a hundred tons in weight – had been processed at Grytviken. Even a twenty-foot blue whale, cut up and weighed for Kohl-Larsen's assiduous notebook, yielded 9,116 kg of blubber, 25,940 kg of meat and 9,433 kg of bone. The heart alone weighed 329 kg (nearly a third of a ton).

The Christian Salvesen company, operating at Leith and Stromness, had already developed the technique of extracting every last ounce of oil, fertiliser and animal feed from the whales' meat and skeletons, and the Falklands government had made this mandatory at all the stations. But in the profligate early days, and during the First World War when regulations were relaxed, carcasses had been abandoned after stripping just the valuable blubber and baleen. Whole skeletons had washed ashore and now in 1928 Kohl-Larsen was appalled, walking round the beach beyond Grytviken, to find that 'the bones of whales lay piled in great heaps, while the rocky section of the beach displayed a yellowish-brown coating derived from rotting whale offal slippery with oil and highly unaesthetic'.

On the flensing plan itself, where a whale could be cut up in under an hour, the carnage was grotesque. In 1914 George Hurley, the celebrated Australian photographer to Shackleton's expedition, waiting to sail south on the ill-fated voyage into the Weddell Sea, recorded delicious dinners of roast pork with the station commander. The Grytviken pigs were fed on whale meat and one afternoon Hurley and his friends 'observed a herd of the said whale-fed pigs emerging from a hole in the side of a highly-odorous whale, where they had just revelled, judging by their grunts of repletion, in a sumptuous gorge. The sight completely upset the more susceptible members of the expedition who refused all further invitation to dine ashore.'

Hunting the world's greatest mammal to the edge of extinction to feed domestic animals to feed humans . . . it seems a horrible perversion but animal feed was, of course, only a by-product. Most valuable was the blubber and, with those non-toothed species that feed on the shrimp-like krill, baleen – the plates of so-called 'whalebone' used to trap the krill in the whale's mouth as it expels water. Before the invention of plastic baleen had a thousand applications, most famously for making corsets; but the bulk product came from the great insulating layer of blubber, common to all whales, toothed and baleen. At first the oil rendered from whale blubber was used mainly for low grade heating and lighting fuel, but in 1906 the invention of hydrogenation, the process for turning the oil into a hard fat, elevated it to a multi-purpose raw material. Soap and margarine were the most obvious products, but there was also a range of specialised medical products, and industrial lubricants and, from 1914 to 1918, a massive demand for the by-product used to make nitro-glycerine. Whale oil prices soared during the Great War and production on South Georgia reached a new peak during the 1915–16 season.

Prices dropped immediately after the Armistice, but later picked up again so that whaling continued to flourish on South Georgia. From the 1920s there was competition from floating factory ships working the icy waters further south, but the ships needed the back-up of shore bases, which in any case were more economical and efficient than floating factories for processing any whales caught close to the island. However, by the 1930s it was already apparent that the summer whale population was starting to dwindle. Efforts by the Falklands government, and later the International Whaling Commission, to conserve stocks failed. Finally, in 1963, the two companies still operating on South Georgia, Christian Salvesen and Albion Star (formerly Compañía Argentina de Pesca), admitted that there were not enough whales left to make the industry profitable. Grytviken and Leith Harbour were sub-leased for another two years to Japanese companies, but even those determined exploiters of the ocean managed in the final year to catch only 239 whales, a pathetic fraction of the 1925–6 record catch of 7825. Leith Harbour closed in December 1965; Grytviken in 1964.

Now, walking around the Grytviken station twenty-five years

later, I felt melancholic. Apart from the ruthless slaughter of the whales, there was something rather depressing about man's subsequent vandalism. In the hydro-electric generator house water gushed from smashed turbines and the walls were spattered with bullet holes. The two remaining sealing vessels were scuttled. Smashed windows, graffiti and heaps of tangled rubbish on the jetty were further signatures of bored tourists, fishermen and soldiers on the rampage. But in spite of the vandalism it was not hard to imagine the station in its heyday, with several hundred men working shifts around the clock. We saw the men's sleeping barracks, the manager's house and the storeroom, the chicken house and piggery, the football pitch where Grytviken would play visiting teams from Leith, Stromness or Husvik, the cinema and the graveyard.

One echoing great hangar of a building was still full of cast iron machinery, much of it stamped proudly with names of great manufacturers from Leeds, Birmingham and Stockton. Grytviken employed a full-time staff of marine engineers equipped with machine shops, lifting gear, plate rollers, spare parts and a floating dock. In 1939, when HMS *Exeter* limped away from Montevideo harbour, badly damaged after the battle with the German battleship *Graf Spee*, she tried to effect repairs at Port Stanley but eventually it was here, at this secluded harbour on South Georgia, that she was able to refit while the injured crewmen were treated at the whalers' hospital.

One evening I visited the Scandinavian church, the most southerly church in the world. Amidst all the rusting desolation, the British garrison has taken pride in maintaining the building, repainting the white weatherboarded exterior and keeping the pine pews inside in perfect condition. On one side of the altar a bronze bust commemorates Grytviken's founder, Captain Larsen. On the other side I found a wheezy old harmonium and couldn't resist sitting down to play it. It was hardly an appropriate instrument and the harder I pumped on the creaking foot pedals the further back my flimsy chair slid from the keyboard. But I relished the absurdity of it, crashing my way very badly, arms at full stretch, through a Mozart piano concerto I had learned at school twenty years earlier.

Living quarters and the niceties of life were kept on the periphery at Grytviken. People had to be housed, fed, entertained and (when Larsen had his way) evangelised; but their ultimate purpose was to hunt and process whales. The site is still dominated by two great clusters of rusting storage tanks – petroleum fuel on one side and whale oil on the other – which frame the huge factory complex. Every summer until 1964 the tall chimneys belched steam from specialised boilers lined up in the blubber, meat and bone cookeries and guano factory. But the visible heart of the operation, feeding the cookers, was the flensing plan – a huge wooden deck sloping gently up from the shore.

Duncan Carse had shown us his pictures of inflated whale carcasses floating in King Edward Cove, waiting to be winched up on to the flensing plan. Once the carcass was on the plan the men set to with long flensing knives, shaped like hockey sticks, stripping the skin and blubber and carving it into small enough pieces for the blubber cookers. Then the flesh was stripped and cut up for the meat cookers. That left the skeleton, perhaps eighty or ninety feet long, to be winched up a central ramp to the upper deck. The wooden planking was now rotten and mossy, but Julian and I climbed carefully up the side of the ramp to the top deck where the steel boiler lids were now firmly rusted in place. Thirty years earlier they would have hinged open to swallow lengths of rib and great hunks of vertebrae, sliced into sections by steam-powered saws, so that they too could yield the last drop of oil before being ground down to bonemeal fertiliser.

I think it was the giant rusty sawblade, its vicious teeth silhouetted against the calm turquoise of Cumberland Bay, that symbolised most starkly the ruthless efficiency of the industry. All of us were moved but Julian reacted the most emotionally and was primed for a confrontation with the surviving representatives of the industry, the men from Christian Salvesen, which since 1979 has leased all the derelict stations. They had just started their assessment of Grytviken and, together with Nigel Bonner, were busily taking notes on the dangerous state of some of the buildings. The Salvesen men did not seem very talkative, but when Julian muttered, 'Horrible, murderous business, wasn't it?' Nigel Bonner, hoping perhaps for a good reaction, retorted cheerfully,

'It's no different from killing chickens.'

If one wants to be ruthlessly objective, perhaps there is a very good case for saying that cutting up whales on South Georgia was no different from sending domestic animals to the abattoir. But Bonner would be the first to agree that harvesting a wild creature like the whale whilst failing to conserve stocks was a disaster by even the most objective criteria. If, like Julian, and probably most of us, you allow emotional and aesthetic considerations to enter the argument, the disaster is amplified. Later that summer one poignant story removed any doubts I had about the cruelty of whaling.

Captain Ian Gemmell was one of the Green Howards officers at the garrison. During his four months at King Edward Point he took a keen interest in the whaling station and one of his jobs, when occasional Antarctic cruise ships called in, was to show passengers round Grytviken. One batch of visitors that year included an English ex-whaler, now in his mid-fifties, revisiting the waters he had worked as a young man. He told Ian about the occasion when, as his catcher 'played' a mortally wounded whale on the harpoon cable, the victim's mate hung around, obviously distressed, watching the death agonies of its spouse. Once the harpooned whale died it was inflated and left floating with the customary marker flag, ready for towing back to the factory later.

The surviving whale had now fled, but the ship raced off at 20 knots in pursuit. The captain was determined to add another animal to that day's catch, so he followed relentlessly the tell-tale spume each time the quarry had to surface and blow. The chase lasted nineteen hours. The man told Ian how, during that endless chase, his adrenaline rush of excitement gradually subsided to hollow regret as he witnessed the whale's desperate fight for survival. Eventually, utterly exhausted, the whale changed direction in a final effort to escape, but this allowed the ship to close in and fire the lethal harpoon.

Later that afternoon we walked up to the fenced enclosure of the Grytviken cemetery. The largest gravestone was a rough granite block engraved with the words: *To the dear memory of Sir Ernest Shackleton, Explorer, Born 15th February 1874 – Entered Life*

Eternal 5th January 1922. Most of the other graves were marked with small crosses or plaques commemorating Anderssens, Amundsens, Olsens and a Fredikson who was only twenty-one when he died in 1912, one of several victims of a typhoid epidemic. Then there was the Magistrate who was caught in an avalanche on the narrow road linking King Edward Point and Grytviken. The most recent cross marked the remains of Felix Artuso, the Argentinian submariner killed on April 26, 1982.

Artuso was the only man to die during the British recapture of South Georgia and his death was the result of a stupid misunderstanding, but several Argentinians had died during their fierce battle to take the island three weeks earlier. Half a mile round the coast from the cemetery we found the remains of the Puma helicopter shot down by the Royal Marines. Souvenir hunters had stripped all the controls and only the bare hulk remained, riddled with bullet holes and scrawled graffiti. British thuggery was celebrated by: *Taff Kenny – CARDIFF CITY, LFC Rules, Fuck off Argies* and *WERE's* [sic] *THE ARGIES NOW THEN.* Some German tourist, with no axe to grind, had just engraved passionately, *Wolfi – Trudi.*

On that summer afternoon it was hard to believe that only seven years earlier this peaceful cove had witnessed one of the most bizarre battles in modern history; but the shot-down helicopter, Artuso's grave and the soldiers now guarding the island, with their defensive dugouts around Shackleton House, were reminders that there really had been fighting here. Argentina's claim to the Falkland Islands Dependencies was based on some fairly spurious interpretations of history. On South Georgia itself those claims can be traced back to the year 1904, when Captain Larsen founded the first whaling station at Grytviken.

5

Operation Paraquat

The background to the 1982 crisis is a tortuous story of bluff and counter-bluff, rival claims, ambiguous treaties and occasional scuffles, played out in an elaborate diplomatic game, often co-operative, sometimes antagonistic, dating back to the Napoleonic Wars.

In 1806 a British force attacked the Spanish settlement at Buenos Aires. It was a private venture without official authority. Nevertheless the British government, seriously concerned at Napoleon's threat to her trading empire in the East, was looking at new strategic areas from which to maintain her maritime domination. So, when a second force attacked Buenos Aires in 1807, it had the full authority of the government. The attempt to establish a presence in South America by force was defeated, but in subsequent years Britain worked assiduously, by more subtle means, to gain influence in the area. After 1815 a strong naval force remained in the South Atlantic, standing back to watch Spain lose hold of her South American empire. Then in 1825, with an eye to the main chance, Britain signed a treaty of friendship with the new independent United Provinces of Rio del Plata. British capital and technology were poured into what was to be Argentina; British settlers established successful industries and farming *estancias*; the Royal Navy protected the emergent nation and policed its maritime trade.

During this period the last French, Spanish and Latin American settlers left the Falkland Islands and in 1833 Britain established formal administration there. British Letters Patent, providing for the government of the 'Falkland Islands Dependencies', were published in 1843, 1876 and 1892, but the precise extent of the dependencies was not stated. Sovereignty of South Georgia, 750 miles to the east, had been assumed since Cook's landing in 1775, but in practice the island had been the domain of lawless sealers, mainly American. The Sealing Ordinances of 1881, aimed at regulating the industry, had little effect. In any case, the fur seal was by now nearly extinct, and the elephant seals seriously depleted. But in 1900, hopeful of exploiting possible alternative economic resources, Britain invited tenders for commercial leases on South Georgia. Three years later the invitation was taken up by a consortium of Chilean sheep ranchers; but already Captain Larsen had realised that the really promising resource was the teeming whale population in and around the island's bays.

The British Colonial Office first heard about Larsen's Compañía Argentina de Pesca from newspaper reports. By that time, December 1904, the illegal Argentinian-backed company was already in operation at Grytviken, whilst the Chilean entrepreneurs, complete with formal lease from the British government, had a temporary base nearby on Hestesletten – the 'Horse Plain' where they were grazing their sheep on the tussock grass. The Chileans were understandably upset and demanded exclusive rights to the island, but in 1905 Larsen, aware now of concern in London, applied formally for a lease. The Colonial Office in London was keen to accept the request; but just to emphasise sovereignty, the Commander-in-Chief of the British South Atlantic Fleet was ordered the following January to despatch HMS *Sappho* to Grytviken, in a classic piece of gunboat diplomacy.

For the first time, a warship anchored in Cumberland East Bay and the captain, seeing that Larsen's company was competently run, clinched the Colonial Office decision to grant him a lease. So the Argentinian-registered company acquired legal status on the island, on the clear understanding that the lease had been granted by the British government. Two years later, in 1908, Letters Patent at last defined the precise extent of the Falkland Islands Dependencies. The Falklands themselves lie on the South American continental shelf, only 300 miles east of Argentina. But the dependencies also included the remote oceanic islands of Scotia Ridge, the submarine continuation of the Andes which sweeps in a great arc east then back west to the Antarctic Peninsula. Britain claimed all the islands on the ridge: the Shag Rocks, South Georgia and the even remoter archipelagos of the South Sandwich, South Orkney and South Shetland islands. Finally the dependencies included Grahamland – the portion of the Antarctic continent lying between longitudes 20 and 80 degrees west.

The new Letters Patent were published in the Falkland Islands Gazette and a copy was sent to the Argentinian Foreign Ministry. It was formally acknowledged without protest in 1909, the same year a British Magistrate was installed on South Georgia at King Edward Point.

The Magistrate was policeman, harbourmaster and customs officer for the island. He was also the postmaster and over the years South Georgia stamps became highly prized by collectors, accounting for a significant revenue; but strangely, it was this idiosyncratic by-product of British rule that incurred the first serious challenge, in 1927, when Argentina notified the International Postal Union that South Georgia and the South Orkney Islands should be regarded as Argentinian territory. However, it was not until the 1940s and 1950s that the conflict became more serious. By now both Argentina and Chile were laying claim to the Antarctic mainland, with territories overlapping Britain's Grahamland claim. On one occasion the Argentinian navy prevented British scientists from landing at their scientific base at Hope Bay. Fortunately conflict was averted by the Antarctic Treaty, drafted in 1959 and ratified in 1962 by the twelve nations, including Britain, Chile and Argentina, who then operated scientific bases in Antarctica.

The Antarctic Treaty was a Utopian exercise in international relations which has now operated with remarkable success for thirty years. The twelve original signatories agreed to forgo any military operations in Antarctica, reserving the continent for peaceful science, with a ban on all nuclear activity; they also agreed to freeze all claims to sovereignty. The treaty covered all land and sea south of the 60th parallel, thereby nullifying Britain's claims to the South Orkneys, South Shetlands and Grahamland. Those areas were re-defined as 'British Antarctic Territory', with purely scientific bases operated by the British Antarctic Survey; the islands north of the 60th parallel – the South Sandwich Islands,

South Georgia, the Shag Rocks and the Falklands – remained the 'Falkland Islands Dependencies' – British sovereign territory.

During the Fifties and Sixties HMS *Protector* patrolled the South Atlantic as the guardship of the Falkland Islands and in 1968 that role was assumed by HMS *Endurance*. At first the *Endurance* was virtually unarmed, but during the summer of 1976–7 two events prompted the Admiralty to replace the ship's Whirlwind helicopters with Wasps capable of launching missiles. (By 1989 the Wasps had been superseded by Lynxes.) The first event was Argentina's establishment of a naval base on Southern Thule in the South Sandwich Islands; the second was more blatantly provocative. Lord Shackleton, son of Sir Ernest, was visiting South Georgia as part of his fact-finding mission to prepare a report on the future of the Falklands. He was on board the *Endurance* but the research ship RRS *Shackleton* was also in the area. The captain of an Argentinian destroyer, assuming that the peer was on board the eponymous ship, fired a shot across the bows of the *Shackleton* in an attempt to deter the visit. No one was hurt, and Lord Shackleton continued to prepare his report, but it was another of many signals that Argentina had serious designs on the area.

This was the background when Nick Barker took over as captain of the *Endurance* in 1980. During his first season in the south he made a point of immersing himself in the whole military, diplomatic, scientific and economic situation in the South Atlantic and Antarctica. He talked to a physicist embarked on a German survey ship anchored off Deception Island, near the Antarctic Peninsula and was told, 'Soon we will have a bigger ship and a base here. We think there are minerals and hydrocarbons.' Barker now agrees with the consensus that to develop oil fields within the Antarctic Treaty area could be an environmental catastrophe; but ten years ago 'it first opened my eyes to what sort of threat there was from Japan and Germany . . . with no indigenous oil of their own. It was listening to them that made me feel it absolutely necessary to keep tabs on what other countries are doing in the area.'

With the whole future of Antarctica in the balance, Barker was convinced that Britain should maintain a credible naval presence, separate from the British Antarctic Survey ships, *Bransfield* and *John Biscoe*, which were fully occupied servicing the British scientific bases. But it was north of the 60th parallel, in British sovereign territory, that he was most concerned. On a friendly visit to an Argentinian air base, talking casually with one of the helicopter pilots, he discovered that Argentina was operating offshore oil rigs up to 100 miles east of the mainland. If Argentina could exploit this resource, why not the Falklands government, too? He also drew attention to the potential for fishing, predicting correctly that there must be valuable fishing grounds around the Falklands.

The *Endurance* routinely kept tabs on the movements of all ships in the area. Given the tiny volume of shipping and the tradition of sharing meteorological information, it was quite easy to listen in to all radio traffic. Spanish-speaking radio operators monitored Argentinian radio broadcasts, but Barker also made a point of making his own assessments. The bright red Plum, less threatening than a heavily armed grey frigate, had always received a warm reception in South American ports and it was normal to entertain Argentinian officers on board. Barker also had close friends in Buenos Aires and during his first season south their remarks convinced him that Britain should demonstrate a stronger will if she wanted to hold on to the Falklands.

In February 1981 an Argentinian oil rig tender was discovered anchored without permission in one of the remote bays of West Falkland. A thousand miles to the south-east the Argentinian navy maintained its naval base in the South Shetlands, but the British government forbade Barker to interfere, preferring to turn a blind eye to the base on Southern Thule. 'They said that it was virtually on the 60th parallel, so we might as well treat it as lying within the Antarctic Treaty area. But I argued: either it's in Antarctica, in which case I must be allowed to visit peacefully what should be a purely scientific base; or it's British sovereign territory, in which case they shouldn't be there at all.'

Nick Barker returned from his first tour south to become a thorn in the flesh of the British establishment. His military status precluded him from joining SWAG – the South West Atlantic Group – a pressure group led by Lord Shackleton and other highly respected Antarctic experts like Sir Peter Scott, Lord Buxton and Sir Vivian Fuchs – but he shared their concerns about the British government's apparent desire to wash her hands of the Falklands. The Defence Secretary, John Nott, forced to trim expenditure to finance the new Trident missile system, had announced in private that the *Endurance*, then costing just £3 million a year, would probably be scrapped at the end of the next season.

Barker recalls that Lord Shackleton asked to meet him just before speaking on the South Atlantic in the House of Lords. The conversation went something like this:

'Could you fill me in on a few details? Has your ship been axed?'

'I can't answer that question. Why don't you ask in the Lords tonight?'

'You're telling me she has?'

'No, I did not say that.'

Barker attended the debate that night where 'by innuendo, it became quite clear that the ship was to be scrapped.' It was at that time that Michael Power, a senior civil servant serving with the Naval Staff and concerned with the Foreign Affairs branch of the Ministry of Defence, reprimanded Barker for straying outside his purely military role as a naval captain. At the end of the year and during the early months of 1982, when Barker was back in the South Atlantic sending increasingly dire warnings to London, they were intercepted by Power, 'who assumed that it was just Nick Barker trying to keep his ship alive'.

Sir Rex Hunt, the Governor of the Falkland Islands, shared Barker's fears. But he too was something of a rebel, unpopular with his Foreign Office bosses who preferred to put their trust in the British Ambassador in Buenos Aires, Sir Anthony Williams. Williams blithely ignored all the warnings that an Argentinian attack was imminent and, as Barker recalls, 'Whatever was sent to London by Rex or myself was almost inevitably countered by Williams.'

When the *Endurance* arrived in the South Atlantic at the start of what was supposed to be her last tour of duty there was little sign of impending trouble. In November 1981 she visited Brazil, Uruguay and Argentina, where the ship's officers and ratings enjoyed the usual round of parties and visits with their Argentinian counterparts. She then steamed east to the Falklands and on to South Georgia where a joint services expedition was landed in Royal Bay. Sir Rex Hunt was on board and later that day, December 12th, Captain Barker ordered one of the Wasp helicopters to land the Governor and his wife at St Andrew's Bay to visit Cindy Buxton and Annie Price, who were filming the penguins there. The helicopter was caught in one of South Georgia's unpredictable wind gusts and crashed on the beach. Luckily no one was hurt but the helicopter was written off.

The helicopter crisis inevitably engendered urgent radio conversations over the next few days – the sort of radio traffic which would normally prompt any other ships in the area to offer help. But it was only when Barker returned to the Falklands at Christmas that he heard that an Argentinian naval vessel, *Almirante Irizar*, had just anchored secretly at Leith Harbour, South Georgia, in radio silence, without seeking permission from the Magistrate at King Edward Point.

The *Almirante Irizar* was captained by Caesar Trombetta. Trombetta had discussed his schedule with Barker in November and made no mention of South Georgia. As Barker discovered during subsequent events, 'Trombetta had told me a pack of lies.' On board the *Almirante Irizar* was Constantino Davidoff, the industrialist who, back in 1978, had approached Christian Salvesen for permission to salvage machinery and valuable scrap metal from the whaling stations. He had a contract for the work but this reconnaissance, landing secretly from a naval vessel, was a clear breach of international law.

The *Endurance* sailed to Uruguay after Christmas to collect a replacement helicopter, then spent the first three weeks of 1982 on scientific work off the Antarctic Peninsula. Then in the last week of January she sailed for the second time that season up the Beagle Channel. This time Barker had a frosty reception from the Argentinians. He was tailed by gunboats and at the Ushuaia naval base he was warned that he was 'in a war zone'. Hints from the Argentinians, soon confirmed by the Chilean navy at Punta Arenas, made it quite clear that 'war zone' referred not just to the recurrent Beagle Channel dispute between Chile and Argentina, but also to the Argentinian Junta's designs on 'Las Malvinas'.

On the 16th March the *Endurance* was back at South Georgia, anchored off King Edward Point. Since his illegal visit in December, Constantino Davidoff had been trying repeatedly to clear his South Georgia salvage operation with the British Foreign Office. Now he was approaching South Georgia in another naval ship, again keeping radio silence. Barker had to return passengers to the Falklands and the Argentinians waited until *Endurance* had sailed before anchoring in Leith Harbour to disembark salvage workers, soldiers and equipment.

For many years now the administration of South Georgia had been the responsibility of the British Antarctic Survey, which maintained the base at King Edward Point and isolated huts around the island. During the next two weeks it was the civilian base commander and official Magistrate of the island, Steve Martin, who kept London informed through an elaborate system of radio messages, relayed between the British Antarctic Survey, the Falklands' Governor, HMS *Endurance* and the Foreign Office. While Steve Martin delivered the official British protest to Leith Harbour, the *Endurance* was ordered back to South Georgia to disembark a detachment of twenty-two Royal Marines at King Edward Point. Captain Trombetta was also back at the island, this time in another armed naval ship, the *Bahía Paraíso* and further warships, including the Exocet-fitted *Guerrico*. The *Endurance*, Britain's sole naval ship in the South Atlantic, was now very vulnerable and when Barker was ordered to leave South Georgia yet again on 31st March and return to the crisis in the Falklands, he knew that Trombetta was waiting for him at the mouth of Cumberland Bay.

The *Endurance*, slow, unwieldy, lightly armed and painted bright red, could hardly have been less suited to the cat and mouse games of the next few weeks; but her company knew the South Georgia coastline better than most and their captain was determined to evade the enemy. All lights were extinguished and the ship kept radar and radio silence as she sailed that night up the east coast of the bay, hugging close to the rocks and sneaking out of the bay through a very narrow passage between rock shoals.

Merton Passage was only sketchily surveyed. In the darkness

Barker could see breakers on both sides passing very close and at one point the ship only cleared the shoreline by twenty feet. It was very risky but his bold move worked; he rounded the headland undetected, continued down the north-east coast, round Cape Disappointment and out into the safety of the open sea.

Two days later Argentinian troops landed on the Falklands before the *Endurance* could get back to Stanley. The following day, April 3rd, South Georgia was taken, but not without a fierce battle killing several Argentinians. Unknown to Trombetta, twenty-two Royal Marines were dug into trenches around Shackleton House, while the British Antarctic Survey civilians took shelter at Grytviken church. For several hours the Marines held off the attack, shooting down the troop-carrying Puma helicopter which crash-landed on the far side of the cove, and resisting bombardment from two warships. Eventually, vastly outnumbered, they had to surrender and the Argentinian flag was hoisted at King Edward Point.

The Argentinian invasion was allowed to happen by a dismal failure of British foreign and military policy; but once the blunder was realised, the government responded with remarkable speed and efficiency. Even while the Marines and BAS personnel were being taken prisoner at King Edward Point, the first military transports were setting off from Britain, 8000 miles away. By April 7th the secret decision had been made to mount 'Operation Paraquat', ordering HMS *Plymouth*, HMS *Antrim* and RFA *Tidespring* to separate from the main Falklands Task Force with detachments of Royal Marines, SBS and SAS soldiers, hurry south, rendezvous with HMS *Endurance* and continue to South Georgia. By April 20th the four ships were in position off the island.

Britain was still not officially at war with Argentina and the commanders of Operation Paraquat had been ordered to retake South Georgia with minimal damage to life and property. Denied the easy option of blanket bombardment, they had to use stealth and cunning against an enemy whose numbers and defences were unknown. In fact the Argentinians had made a very poor job of defending their new territory. However, as the Commander of British Land Forces, Major Guy Sheridan, pointed out, 'I had to go on the assumption that they had covered themselves thoroughly, with lookouts commanding and covering all the likely landing areas.' That dictated sending reconnaissance parties to assess the enemy's positions at King Edward Point and at Leith Harbour, further west.

The operation had to be coordinated from the heaving decks of four different ships battered by almost continuous gales. Winter was approaching, with the additional hazard of icebergs. On the island itself, deep snow and whiteout blizzard conditions would make any serious overland travel extremely dangerous. While the *Endurance* inserted SBS men to the east of Grytviken, the SAS decided on a wild plan for the Leith reconnaissance, insisting that if helicopters came within ten miles of the whaling station the Argentinians would be alerted. So, against his better judgment, Sheridan agreed reluctantly to the SAS mountain troop's plan to land right up on the Fortuna Glacier, nearly fifteen miles west of Leith. They were landed successfully, but that day they only made half a mile across the glacier, pulling each other out of crevasses every few yards. They were trying to repeat the final part of Shackleton's epic traverse to Stromness Bay, but in 1916 Shackleton had been blessed with almost perfect weather. On this occasion conditions were atrocious; the tents were ripped to shreds and after a night huddled in snow trenches on the glacier, all the soldiers were soaked and getting dangerously close to hypothermia. In the morning their leader had no choice but to radio the ships for a rescue. The Fortuna Glacier was now a maelstrom of swirling whiteness, with visibility down to a few yards and wind gusting to nearly 100 knots. During the rescue, two Wessex helicopters crashed on the glacier, but incredibly no one was hurt and a third helicopter finally evacuated everyone safely.

The next approach to Leith was made by sea. Again it was a bold operation, involving HMS *Antrim* sailing into the vulnerable enclosure of Stromness Bay and launching five inflatable boats in the pitch blackness of a stormy night. Three crafts just made it to Grass Island to establish an observation point, but the other two were driven out to sea, when their outboard motors failed. The crew of *Delta* just managed to paddle themselves on to Busen Point where they went to ground, but *Bravo* was swept past into the open sea and headed west for Australia.

At dawn the overworked Wessex helicopter was launched from *Antrim* to search a huge storm-swept tract of ocean in lousy visibility, without the benefit of radar, for fear of alerting the Argentinians, and at the extreme end of its endurance located *Bravo* and rescued the three frightened occupants.

Meanwhile the SBS soldiers were having their own problems further down the coast, opposite King Edward Point. The *Endurance* had landed them on the far shore of the Barff Peninsula, enabling them to walk unobserved over the peninsula to the shore of Cumberland East Bay. The plan from there was to cross the bay and Moraine Fjord by night and land close to King Edward Point to assess the enemy's defences. But once again the island defeated them with its own defences, long before they got anywhere near the Argentinians. This time it was ice – bergs, growlers and brash ice churning the water and nearly crushing the tiny inflatable boats. After several attempts the men had to admit defeat and return to the *Endurance*.

Mountain warfare is a dangerous, haphazard business. In the First World War thousands of German and Italian troops were killed by avalanches in the Dolomites, with only minimal territorial gains on either side. The French Chasseurs Alpins in the Second World War achieved little real advantage against the Germans; and the recent war between India and Pakistan on the Siachen Glacier has dragged on for several years in dangerous, ridiculous stalemate. On South Georgia, Operation Paraquat had to contend with all the hazards of mountain terrain, and the difficulties of a risky amphibious operation, approaching through the stormiest seas in the world, in winter. The reconnaissance missions were hardly a resounding success, but it seems remarkable that not a single life was lost in the attempt, and the whole operation was kept secret until the last moment.

Things came to a head on April 24th in a farcical scene that seems to epitomise the essential ridiculousness of war. Argentinian Hercules aircraft had flown over South Georgia the previous day, the British task force was losing the advantage of secrecy and now an Argentinian Boeing 707 was flying another reconnaissance mission over the island. It was a clear day and the *Endurance* was sitting like a bright red beacon, plainly visible in Hound Bay. Nick Barker was talking on the satellite to the British Chief of Staff, 8000 miles away in a bunker in North London, who had already warned of the presence of an Argentinian submarine. His gunners were on deck manning the Oerlikons, but the official order was not to fire unless the enemy offered a direct threat! Barker was monitoring Argentinian radio calls and could clearly hear the Spanish-speaking voices giving instructions to the Argentinian submarine. He knew quite well that if his ship was torpedoed no one would survive in the Antarctic water for more than a few minutes.

Barker held the telephone receiver into the radio office, for the benefit of his superiors, then spoke himself to London: 'Hear that, sir? That racket is my ship going to action stations. We have an Argentinian aircraft overhead. The pilot is talking plain language to a submarine, telling him where I am and what I am doing. I really do think I should land my special forces as soon as possible.'

The Chief of Staff reassured Barker that central command in London had a better overview of the situation and reiterated the order not to fire unless provoked. They did, however, give him permission to land his special forces. Barker later discovered that the submarine, the *Santa Fe*, had actually been loitering outside Hound Bay at that very moment and at one stage the commanding officer had had his periscope trained on the *Endurance*. Two days later, when Barker asked Captain Bicain why he hadn't fired, the Argentinian replied, 'I think it must have been that excellent cocktail party you gave us at Mar del Plate last November.'

The British were finally given permission to fire the next morning, April 25th. By now HMS *Brilliant* had reinforced the operation and in a series of missile and depth charge attacks, helicopters from *Brilliant*, *Plymouth*, *Antrim* and *Endurance* crippled the *Santa Fe* just outside Cumberland Bay. On the final attack one of the *Endurance* Wasps shadowed the submarine right to the jetty at King Edward Point. Taking advantage of the Argentinian confusion, Guy Sheridan pressed for an immediate attack and the naval commander in the *Antrim*, Captain Young, agreed. The navy started a demoralising creeping bombardment from the open sea, lobbing shells across the Barff Peninsula and

Cumberland East Bay, to explode on Hestesletten, the flat shelf of tussock grass just south of Grytviken.

Soon the bombardment was shifted closer to King Edward Point, enabling the soldiers to land at Hestesletten. The main body of Sheridan's M Company was 250 miles out to sea on *Tidespring* so he had to make do with a scratch force, as he confided later that day in his diary: 'I had 75 men – about half of the opposition I expected. So it was a gamble.' It was also something of a shambles, with the SAS rushing on ahead: 'At one point they opened fire on a colony of elephant seals. God, what a lot of cowboys they are.'

It was only when the attackers came round the crest of Brown Mountain and looked down into the cove that they saw the white flag flying at King Edward Point. Demoralised by the naval bombardment, the occupying force at King Edward Point had surrendered with hardly a murmur of protest; but now, nearly eight years later, looking across the cove from the Grytviken cemetery, one hardly needed military expertise to understand why the British had approached with such caution in 1982. The entrance to Cumberland East Bay, which we had sailed through in the *Endurance* that morning, is only three miles wide and the inner sanctuary of King Edward Cove itself is just half a mile across, encircled by high hills that could have been riddled with gun posts. Guy Sheridan had every reason to expect snipers amongst the warren of derelict buildings at Grytviken and from there the only way of advancing to the Point was along the narrow road which curves round the cove beneath steep scree slopes and cliffs.

Once King Edward Point had been dealt with, it only remained to get a formal surrender from the Argentinian salvage workers and soldiers twelve miles away at Leith. The commander there, Teniente de Navio Astiz, only agreed to surrender reluctantly after several long talks on the radio with Nick Barker. The following morning, after sailing round to Stromness Bay, Barker arranged to land a helicopter on the football pitch to accept Astiz's formal surrender. Recalling that morning, Barker spoke very quietly: 'I'm not sure quite why, but I suddenly felt uneasy about it and decided not to go in with the helicopter. So I changed the plan and ordered Astiz to walk out with all his men on to the harbour front.'

The captains of the *Endurance* and *Plymouth* watched from their ships as the Argentinians emerged from the buildings at Leith to be searched by SAS and SBS men. Afterwards, the SAS demolition experts inspected the football pitch and found, buried beneath the large 'H' marking the proposed helicopter landing spot, a steel barrel packed with high explosives and scrap metal. Barker later discovered that Astiz had been used by the Junta, and was wanted by the governments of Sweden and France in connection with the disappearance of their nationals in Argentina.

While the prisoners were being rounded up at Leith and King Edward Point, on board *Antrim* the captain showed Sheridan a signal from CinCfleet: 'Recommendations for awards for gallantry to be signalled immediately.' Sheridan recorded drily in his diary, 'I solemnly told him that "they must be joking". When no shots had been fired against us, how on earth could I make a gallantry recommendation?' Nevertheless, back at home, Margaret Thatcher appeared on the steps of 10 Downing Street, exhorting us all to 'Rejoice!' At the time it seemed unnecessarily jingoistic and few people realised the tactical significance of the victory. Apart from the huge morale boost, retaking South Georgia gave the British Forces a secure forward operating base for the Falklands Task Force. During the next few weeks Cumberland Bay was to be thronged with warships and requisitioned mercantile vessels ranging from Alan Marr's fishing boats to great ocean liners such as the *Canberra* and *Queen Elizabeth II*. Here, in a secure anchorage 700 miles from Argentina and out of range of most of her fighter planes, British ships could transfer troops and supplies, effect repairs and carry out all the other jobs that are virtually impossible on the open sea. Without that strategic advantage, and later the controversial removal of the *Belgrano* threat, the British forces might have had a much harder job retaking the Falklands.

After 1982 South Georgia was brought under the direct administration of the Foreign and Commonwealth Office. The British Antarctic Survey had already been planning to stop its research programme on the main island, just keeping the biological station at Bird Island. Now the job of Magistrate is handled by the commanding officer of the fifty-strong garrison at King Edward

Point. He speaks to CBFFI on the Falklands every day but, as Matt O'Hanlon pointed out to us at dinner, he could not defend the island for long against a serious aggressor. What he can do is maintain a token military presence, demonstrating clearly that Britain intends to hold on to the island. In the event of a serious invasion he could deploy men in the hills around Grytviken, making life difficult for the enemy until British reinforcements arrived.

At the end of 1989, with a new democratic government in Argentina and diplomatic relations about to be renewed with Britain, an attack was highly unlikely but the garrison was there, just in case. As Commanding Officer and Magistrate, Matt was technically responsible for the Southern Ocean Mountaineering Expedition as long as we were on the island. We had stressed all along that we would be almost entirely self-sufficient, but our plan to walk south to our cache at Royal Bay depended on an initial ride across Cumberland East Bay as walking round the head of the inlet would involve a tortuous journey around deep fjords and over chaotic glaciers. Luckily Phil Rotier from the Scott Polar Research Institute was going across the bay next morning to set up a marker pole for his acoustic survey work. There was just room for the five of us and our gear in the *Stanscombe Wills*, and he kindly agreed to let us share the lift.

Our plan was to spend the final part of the expedition at the little hut on the far shore of Cumberland East Bay, where we would leave enough food and fuel for three weeks' use in February; but for the first six or seven weeks we would be down at the southern end of the island, out of sight and radio contact with the garrison. In the event of an accident our medical officer, Brian, could patch up the victim and administer morphine, but somehow we would have to get the casualty back to King Edward Point. If the injury was very serious we would need help, so Matt agreed to deliver emergency flares to a specified point on the Barff Peninsula, from where we could signal King Edward Point in a dire emergency.

Brian had done a crash course in first aid just before leaving Britain, but it was reassuring to know that there was also a qualified medic on the island. Ian Gemmell, the young Green

Howards officer, was the garrison doctor. He had also been delegated the job of postmaster and we kept him busy that evening issuing stamps, counting change and franking our pile of expedition postcards.

This was probably our last chance for weeks to write to friends, helpers and sponsors, and it was my last chance to write a long letter to Rosie. So much had happened in the ten days since our dismal parting at Brize Norton, yet for all that time we had been passive guests of the armed services. Now we would have to start looking after ourselves. For the first time in one and a half years I would have to do some serious mountain walking with a heavy rucksack on my back. Feeling a little apprehensive about all that effort, I finished my letter, had one last whisky and went to bed.

6

The Reindeer Trail

The sea was calm the next morning for our eight-mile boat journey across Cumberland East Bay. The red roofs of King Edward Point receded in the wake and soon we were chugging past Hestesletten, the flat shelf of tussock grass where the Chileans once experimented with sheep grazing and where, eighty years later, British forces were put ashore to start their advance on Grytviken. The Foreign and Commonwealth Office has recently toyed with the idea of building an airstrip on the site. Long may its plans gather dust on the drawing board!

We continued past a reef of kelp tentacles swirling across the entrance to Moraine Fjord. Seeing the chaotic icefalls of the Harker and Hamburg glaciers tumbling into the back of the fjord, we realised how lucky we were to have this lift, bypassing that tortuous stretch of coastline. Then we rounded a headland and saw again the massive front of the Nordenskjöld Glacier, one of several polar ice sheets named after the Swedish explorer. Today it was shining silver and the whole of Cumberland Bay was sparkling in the sun but further inland, 5000 feet up in a sapphire sky, huge lenticular clouds were bent into white waves by the ubiquitous wind.

After the melancholic afternoon at Grytviken, this morning there was a happy holiday atmosphere on the *Stanscombe Wills*, with the five of us crowded on to a pile of rucksacks, storage barrels and film gear, water rushing past the gunwhales and the cliffs and coves of the far shore growing rapidly closer. Soon we made out the little white hut at Sörling Valley and as we approached closer fifteen or twenty reindeer made off up the hill, pausing briefly to turn back and stare at the intruders. The

Norwegians introduced three bucks and seven does in 1911 – the nucleus of a herd to provide sport and meat. Now the reindeer are protected, roaming free and without predators along the ice-free stretch of coast from the Barff Peninsula down to Royal Bay. However, they are cut off from Grytviken by the Nordenskjöld Glacier, just as the Neumayer and Fortuna Glaciers keep a second distinct herd isolated on the hills around Stromness Bay.

The boatman slowed right down to steer carefully through a maze of icebergs that had drifted down from the glacier front and nosed the *Stanscombe Wills* up on to a beach of smooth boulders. Kees and I off-loaded all the baggage while the others walked up past pools of wallowing elephant seals to investigate a corrugated iron storage shed just below the main hut. A few minutes later, amid loud battering, there were shouts of, 'Can't understand . . . it's jammed solid . . . something stuck inside . . . ' By the time we joined them, Julian was rising to the challenge with a large battering ram. Between blows, one could hear mysterious snuffling noises from behind the door.

'Hang on a minute, there's going to be some good footage here. Kees!'

He was already pointing his exposure meter at the door and had the Aaton ready on his shoulder. I rushed back to the beach for the Dog, hurriedly set the recording levels and held up a hand ready to tap the sound synchronisation. We were ready. 'Eviction of seal. Take One. Rolling!'

Julian went at the door with gusto, revelling in a spot of justifiable vandalism. There was a loud crash as the door fell in, followed by silence. Then, encouraged by the odd 'Come on, then,' from Lindsay and Brian's prods with the boathook, a young sea elephant cow lumbered out to the doorway, blinked at the bright light, gave an outraged belch at the film crew and wobbled off into the tussock grass. We never quite discovered how she had managed to jam the door shut, nor what she had thought of the half-eaten army compo rations strewn around the interior, but presumably she would not have survived her incarceration indefinitely.

The boat left and we settled down for a picnic lunch in the sun, and discussed plans. The journey to Royal Bay would take two days with an overnight stop at the hut in St Andrew's Bay. It ought to be straightforward, but we had read the account of Geoffrey Sutton's 1954 expedition – one of the very first mountaineering attempts on South Georgia. Within a few hours of arriving on the island, most of the team were fighting for survival in a raging blizzard and one man had nearly broken his back falling down a crevasse. We had no glaciers to cross yet, but we were not taking any chances with South Georgia's fickle weather and had decided to carry a tent and full survival gear in case we didn't make the St Andrew's Bay hut. All that equipment, the stove and food for the journey meant heavy loads. Then we had to add ten kilos of Aaton camera, the Dog, professional tripod and, heaviest of all, the great steel sphere of the fluid head, which revolves on top for slow panning shots. So, to lighten the loads on the first leg of the journey, Brian, Lindsay, Julian and I set off that afternoon to reconnoitre the route and cache some of the luggage halfway to St Andrew's Bay.

Hints of a path led up Sörling Valley, over a thousand-foot pass and down to the Lönnberg Valley. This was the route over the Barff Peninsula taken by British Antarctic Survey observers and later the Special Boat Squadron in April 1982, on their recces towards King Edward Point. It was a Scottish walk, with low rocky hills, mossy ravines, bog grasses and ever-changing vistas out to sea. But, as we came down into the Lönnberg Valley, Antarctica began to show itself again. Several miles out beyond the mouth of Hound Bay a giant cube of ice drifted by on its slowly disintegrating journey north from one of the Antarctic ice shelves. As we approached the beach I heard voices and an outboard motor, only to realise that it was sea elephants belching. Antarctic terns mobbed us and brown skuas flew in low, swooping at the intruders. A pair of little yellow-billed ducks, South Georgia pintails, flew up from under my feet. Then, as I made my way down the Lönnberg stream looking for a crossing point, I saw our first gathering of little grey and white men, standing rather stiffly on a patch of flattened grass, engaged in the desultory conversation of civil servants at an official garden party. Drawing closer I noticed above their grey tailcoats, out-rageous bright orange collars, and realised that these were the most beautiful of all the penguin species – the king penguin.

The next day we would see the many thousands at the vast St Andrew's Bay colony, but I could not resist stopping to photograph this little group of about fifty birds. Some of the company stood slightly apart at a respectful distance from a cluster of nesting parents. 'Nesting' is of course something of a misnomer, because a king incubator presides over the most imperceptible scrape in the ground, hunched with its protective flap over the single egg resting on its semi-webbed clawed feet.

I was allowed to sit and admire the birds from just a few feet away. James Weddell, the nineteenth-century sealer and polar explorer, wrote that of all birds only the peacock has a more magnificent plumage than the king penguin. Most of this group had recently moulted, revealing brilliant coats.

It is impossible not to anthropomorphise penguins. Niall Rankin, the ornithologist whose 1946–7 expedition was described so engagingly in *Antarctic Isle*, described them all as girls; but I found the king, with its formal attire and vain, pompous manner, exclusively, ridiculously masculine. In fact males and females look identical, with a gleaming white shirt front. The back is silver grey, in the same thick, sleek, water-resistant coating, more like a seal's fur than feathers. The grey coat extends round the shoulders and is gathered up at the chin, over a necktie the colour of the richest egg yoke – deep yellow, fading to paler shades and merging to white as it spills down the shirt front. The tie also extends round the back of the neck, swelling into two yellow lozenges set into the jet black head plumage. Two slivers of pinker orange, set like marquetry into the sides of the long tapered beak, suggest a smile; but the eyes, dark brown with barely perceptible pupils, are quite inscrutable. They are set flush into the side of the head, streamlined for speed underwater. All the power comes from the fish-bird wings, refined to the simplicity of flippers, with feathers reduced to a sleek coating like fish scales.

I spent nearly half an hour admiring the penguins, then continued up the far side of the valley to catch up with the others. About 700 feet up the hillside we left our cache marked by a large cairn, then headed back to Cumberland Bay.

Walking back down Sörling Valley, Julian gazed longingly at

the reindeer, wishing that he had been allowed to bring his beloved 30-06 for a spot of deerstalking, but then admitting that these tame animals would be poor sport and looked pretty scrawny anyway, after years of inbreeding with no predators. Like so many country people, Julian seemed possessed by the strange itch to go out and kill things. I found the idea a little hard to accept, but I was salivating at the memory of the recent farewell dinner in Shropshire, when we had devoured an enormous succulent haunch of venison shot by the fair hand of Our Leader; so any criticism by me would have amounted to rank hypocrisy. In any case Julian's shooting did not alter the fact that, like so many hunters, he had a far greater love and understanding of his own countryside than the average anti-blood-sport leaguer, ranting sanctimoniously from a position of city-bred ignorance. On South Georgia he soon grew accustomed to just looking.

The sun was going down as we returned to Cumberland Bay. Brian, Julian and Lindsay climbed round the back of a headland to reach the hut, but I was in adventure mode and took a direct line around the shore. After a day's easy walking, it was good to traverse rockcliffs above the sea and, when the rocks became blank, to climb up amongst the overhanging fronds of tussock grass, spreading my weight carefully over the tussocks. I found a small gathering of cormorants – the black and white blue-eyed cormorants of South Georgia – sitting on a rock pedestal, only flying off at the last moment when I had to climb past them. Beyond the cliff I bumped into a chinstrap penguin – the only one we saw on the island – strutting busily along the shingle beach. Niall Rankin reported chinstrap or 'ringed' penguin colonies at the far southern end of the island and remarked on the birds' aggressive behaviour. This stray just looked me over, giving me a chance to admire the thin black line etched across his white face, then belly-flopped into the sea and swam away. But curiosity got the better of him and he waddled ashore fifty yards further on, waiting for me to walk really close before he dived into the sea again.

The inspection was repeated several times as I walked along the beach. Eventually, to give him a better look, I stopped and sat down. It was an enchanting moment – the waves lapping the shore, the solitary chinstrap curiously observing me, the cormorants more blasé, sitting further out on a grounded iceberg. Tranquillity, solitude and a sense of rightness – of life following some essential, logical pattern – created one of those rare moments of contentment, heightened probably by the knowledge that in a few minutes I would be back with the others in the hut, enjoying hot supper and a bottle of wine.

The meteorological officer on the *Endurance* had warned us that a big front was approaching South Georgia from Cape Horn. So far we had been blessed with dry weather but the next morning, when we said goodbye to the hut on Cumberland Bay, the sky was heavy with cloud. By the time we were approaching the previous day's cache sleet was scudding across the hillside and the land was shrouded in mist. All the rocks, gullies and snow patches memorised the previous afternoon now looked identical and it took a long time to find the cairn. When we did eventually find it and start sharing out the cache, it was only to curse at all the extra weight that went into our rucksacks.

We trudged on through the cloud. Julian did things with the map and compass while Brian seemed to rely on intuition; between them they kept us pointing in roughly the right direction, sloshing through sodden snow drifts, skidding down scree slopes and eventually descending a boggy valley towards the sea to find ourselves peering over immense cliffs to the waves. The navigation was almost spot on, and after a short traverse round a headland we found ourselves looking down a grass ramp to St Andrew's Bay. Grey rivers meandered down from the receded glaciers across a wide plain of grey sand sloping down to the grey sea. From that dismal scene of desolation there arose a raucous clamour of penguins, squawking and trumpeting above the surge of wind and waves. I began to try to estimate numbers, looking down on the crowds of pale shirt fronts clustered in groups of hundreds, but quickly gave up.

We found the hut about half a mile up from the sea. Like most of the British Antarctic Survey huts on the island, it was a small wooden building, guyed down with half-inch steel cables. We left a pile of dripping clothes in the ante-room and crowded, steaming, into the cosy inner sanctum furnished with three comfortable bunks and a small table. Sitting on the top bunk in dry clean clothes, drinking soup and listening to the rain pouring down the windows outside, I felt profoundly grateful to Cindy Buxton and Annie Price, who had this hut built in 1981. From this comfortable base, the two women spent the summer of 1981–2 making a film about the king penguin colony at the bay. They were probably the first women to do scientific work on the island since Birgit Kohl-Larsen's visit in 1928. That and the fact that Cindy's father, Lord Buxton, was head of Anglia Television might have given them a degree of publicity; being on the island during the Argentinian invasion ensured their elevation to the status of household names.

The two women lived in the tiny hut throughout the crisis and it was here that the *Endurance* helicopter crash-landed in December 1981, the same week that Captain Trombetta made his first illegal landing at Leith. The women stayed on through the rest of the season but three months later, while the *Endurance* was disembarking the Royal Marines to defend King Edward Point, fifteen miles away, they were collected by helicopter for a couple of days' 'R & R' on board the ship before being flown back to their lonely hut. On April 2nd, the day before the Argentinians invaded King Edward Point, the BAS commander, Steve Martin, dispersed as many of his scientists as possible to outlying field huts around the island. Three men, Anthony North, Myles Plant and Peter Stark, were sent to join the two women at St Andrew's Bay. They took the standard route we had now followed and it was on that neck of the Barff Peninsula that they made several recces over the next two weeks to see what the Argentinians were up to.

The British Antarctic Survey was put in an awkward position. The Director, Dr Richard Laws, allowed his network of bases and ships around the Southern Ocean to assist with radio communications, but his civilian organisation had to be seen not to take a direct part in the conflict. On South Georgia the bulk of his employees were taken prisoner at King Edward Point, but the Argentinians never made any attempt to locate the men who remained in isolated field huts.

The BAS personnel left on the island were instructed to lie low and avoid antagonising the enemy but, as BAS has discovered over the years, if you want staff to work for months or even years at a time in the wilds of Antarctica, you have to accept people with a strong spirit of adventure. Anthony North and Myles Plant could not resist a spot of espionage and made several reconnaissance trips on to the Barff Peninsula, ascertaining that the Argentinians had made no attempt to secure that side of Cumberland East Bay. Sadly, their information never got through to Operation Paraquat until they finally met up with the island's liberators in Hound Bay on the night of April 21–2.

It was a filthy night. Some of the SBS men struggled ashore by inflatable boat; others were ferried from the *Endurance* by the flight commander, Tony Ellerbeck, on one of the most risky missions of his career, flying his Wasp close to the waves with neither lights nor radar, blasted and buffeted by vicious katabatic winds. The boat and helicopter parties ended up on opposite sides of the bay, and had to crash their way in the dark through families of protesting seals and penguins before they could rendezvous and make their way to the Hound Bay hut. A light was showing in the window, so while one SBS man knocked nervously on the door, his colleagues took up covering firing position. Instead of Argentinian soldiers they found Anthony North and Myles Plant, who welcomed them into the hut and explained that there were actually no Argentinians this side of Cumberland Bay.

The BAS men returned to St Andrew's Bay the next morning and it was from there that they and the two women heard the naval bombardment start up three days later. Undeterred, Cindy Buxton and Annie Price continued filming the penguins until finally, on April 30th, the St Andrew's party were all airlifted back to the *Endurance*. Eventually, after several ship transfers, they made their way home to Britain.

We did not have the extraneous excitement of distant gunfire, but the second stage of our walk to Royal Bay gave us a day rich in novelty and variety. I was woken at dawn by the noise of elephant seals shuffling and grunting outside and the steady hammering of rain on the hut roof. St Andrew's Bay looked even more desolate than the previous evening and the route around the coast was hidden by cloud, but after breakfast the faint hint of an improvement prompted us to get back into yesterday's wet clothes, shoulder sodden rucksacks, and set off.

Lindsay looked like Moses parting the waves as he picked his way through the penguins. The crowd would shuffle aside, indignant trumpeting heads held high, then close back over the gap as he passed. To avoid wading an icy river we headed half a mile inland on to the sloping tongue of the Heaney Glacier. Even the ice was coated in a slimy layer of dung and moulted feathers, but it was only after getting up on to an old rubble moraine and looking down into a great hollow covering many acres that we saw the main rookery. The whole expanse was mottled grey, white and orange with thousands upon thousands of birds hunched over their eggs. The noise was deafening and the smell resembled a large poultry farm.

King penguins breed on average every one and a half years, so at any time the big colonies are occupied by birds of every age. Above the main rookery we stopped at a nursery area full of semi-mature birds, nearly a year old but still not ready to go to sea. They were as big as the adult nursemaids tending them but were still coated in shaggy brown fur and their voices hadn't broken. The adults trumpet a harsh split note, rather like the klaxons you hear at continental football matches, but these youngsters still piped an innocent shrill whistle, or were comically adolescent, testing their semi-broken voices and proudly displaying gleaming new plumage still half-obsured by tufts of brown bumfluff. One particularly proud ugly duckling had almost completed its transformation and only a punk headcrest of brown fur marred the gleaming perfection of its new incarnation.

The rain had stopped, the sun was shining, and we continued in high spirits down on to the beach, walking below the receded front of the Buxton and Cook glaciers. For the next mile and a half we strode along dry shingle, threading our way through gatherings of penguins and young elephant seals. There were also a few young fur seals, quite different from the lumbering elephants. The thick fur, pointed little ears and whiskered nose; the alternate simpering whine and growling bravado; and the gambolling run on strong, articulate, leather flipper-legs make the fur seal seem engagingly canine; but its sharp teeth are often eager to snap at unwary ankles and adults have been known to inflict serious bites on humans.

They can move very fast on land, despite the handicap of having their back legs tied together, so we were glad of our ski sticks to ward off the more frisky animals.

The teeming beach eventually petered out into a narrow causeway of boulders hemmed in by cliffs. Then we reached a complete impasse where the waves were breaking over the platform. Keener spirits might have retraced their steps and found a way above the cliffs – we stopped for a seaside picnic and waited for the tide to go out.

An hour later we were able to continue, hopping precariously across rockpools. I was poised on a slimy, slippery rock when an unusually big wave crashed over the reef and threw me into a pool, almost dragging me out to sea. Luckily I stayed upright, avoided soaking the £15,000-worth of cine camera in my rucksack, and wrecked only a comparatively cheap compact camera in my pocket.

My dousing provided cheap laughs for the boys and we continued without further excitement along the wave platform to Doris Bay, named, like most of South Georgia's inlets, after one of the many ships that have visited the island. Once again the beach petered out so Julian and I decided to head up on to the hillside to traverse round into the next inlet, Kelp Bay. We followed a precarious reindeer track but it vanished in a shale gully, so we headed back down to the sea. Clambering down through great hanging clumps of tussock grass, Julian stumbled on an albatross nest and called me over to have a look.

They were light-mantled sooty albatrosses, one of the smaller albatross species known collectively as mollyhawks. With a wingspan of just seven feet, they are not as big as the famous wandering albatrosses that live up at the west end of the island, but they are perhaps even more beautiful. The breast and back feathers are a pale, soft, pinky grey; the wings are a darker, bluer grey and the head is charcoal-brown velvet with a thin white rim half-encircling each dark eye; the broad, slightly hooked fishing beak is blackest burnished ebony, with the raised tubular nostrils that give the petrels their label *Tubinares*. One bird was sitting very firmly on its mud eggcup nest whilst two companions stomped around the ledge on outsize flippers, pausing occasionally to examine our cameras and peck tentatively at outstretched hands. We spent twenty enchanting minutes with the birds, took some pictures then made our excuses and slithered down to the beach to meet Lindsay, Brian and Kees.

At Kelp Bay we had to cross a fast-flowing river which knocked Lindsay over, soaking him and wrecking the second camera that day. Any incipient sympathy I felt evaporated later that afternoon, as we headed inland from Kelp Bay, climbing towards the pass that would take us over to Royal Bay. Like most experienced, responsible mountaineers we separated – Brian, Julian and I racing ahead, whilst Kees followed with the dripping Lindsay. The obvious route seemed to follow a snow gully, bang up the head of the valley to the pass, so I set to with enthusiasm, kicking a line of bucket steps up the slope, until Brian offered to take over. Gentlemen that we were, we stopped on the crest of the pass to wait for Lindsay and Kees. We waited and waited. The wind grew fiercer and colder, whipping sleet across the pass. We huddled and shivered behind a rock. Julian, who only two hours earlier had been gurgling in delight at the albatrosses, started to twitch irritably. 'Typical Lindsay! What the hell's he doing?'

'But I told you he's like that,' I retorted smugly. 'You can be quite sure he'll always choose to go a different way from everyone else.' Half an hour later I began to worry that he or Kees might actually be hurt and suggested that we go back to look. Julian was seething with leaderly initiative so we sent him on to start sorting things out at Royal Bay, then we slid reluctantly all the way back down the hard-won snow gully.

There was no sign of Kees and Lindsay in the valley. After ten minutes shouting we climbed laboriously all the way back up to the pass and just as we regained the crest, Lindsay and Kees appeared from behind some boulders.

'Where the hell have you been?'

Lindsay looked his most infuriatingly, disarmingly casual. 'Er, walking up the valley.'

'Well, why the bloody hell didn't you come up the gully?'

'Ah, the gully . . . but the obvious route was up the side of the valley.'

'Bollocks!'

He clearly wasn't going to apologise so I stomped off self-righteously down the far side of the pass, determined to enjoy a little solitude. A long slushy snow gully took me quickly down to the valley floor and the final plod of the day – a glorious Scottish masterpiece of pouring rain, gurgling peaty burns, black rocks and moss beds luminous red and green in the twilight. An hour later I emerged from a little ravine and saw the grey sea spume scudding across Royal Bay. Over on the left, about 400 yards up from the beach, I found the little red hut and a neat row of blue storage barrels. On one of them Ian Abson had scribbled: *Delivered by Endurance Airways*.

Julian was already rummaging in the barrels for our gear and in the fading light we started to erect our largest tent. We were cold and sodden and the wind was screaming down the valley, tearing the flapping tent from our numb hands. Once Brian arrived we had enough manpower to tame the wild beast and soon we had it pitched, with large boulders anchoring the valance all the way round.

Lindsay arrived and the two of us installed ourselves in the large tent, amassing a great pile of sodden clothes in the porch entrance. Julian took up private quarters in his own tent while Kees and Brian laid claim to the two top bunks in the hut. Soon we joined them inside. Dry clothes, a semi-dry hut sheltering us from the howling wind, a hot meal and generous mugs of whisky diffused the afternoon's minor irritations and instilled a convivial glow of team spirit. So far everything had gone to plan, we had reached our destination and, after a day's hard exercise, it only remained to finish the last puff of my evening cigar, drain my whisky mug and sink gratefully into the oblivion of a warm sleeping bag.

7

Sand-blasted at Royal Bay

At Royal Bay we learned about wind. It was not the usual mildly irritating nuisance that we had all experienced in mountains but a new malevolent force, battering mercilessly at our tents, flinging storage barrels across the valley, whipping sand and snow in our faces and, when it got a chance, throwing us bodily to the ground.

Antarctica is like a great centrifuge, spinning clockwise and pushing all the bad weather to the periphery. On the continental plateau high pressure is the norm, with blue skies and minimal precipitation. Although the Antarctic continent holds 90 per cent of all the world's fresh water, as long as it stays frozen the continent is one of the driest places on earth and certain dry valleys can go for years without any precipitation at all. The weather around the coast is much worse and out in the ocean gale-force winds circle the continent almost constantly from west to east. No significant landmass stands in the way of these winds as they blast round the globe, generating the giant waves so feared by sailors in the Roaring Forties, Filthy Fifties and Screaming Sixties. That great spinning mass of air and water is given an extra boost as it gets funnelled through Drake's Passage – the 500-mile gap between Cape Horn and the tip of the Antarctic Peninsula. East of Drake's Passage the westerlies race across the ocean with renewed force and the mountains of South Georgia stand right in their path.

South Georgia's main mountain spine is set more or less at right angles to the prevailing wind. The ridge is at its highest and most continuous in the central Allardyce Range, named after a former Falklands Governor, and the southern Salvesen Range. Most of the mountains are 6000 feet or higher, but there is a break between the two ranges, only 2000 feet above sea level. This mile-wide gap, the Ross Pass, was our proposed gateway to the unclimbed peaks of the Salvesen Range. It was also one of the major wind funnels on the island, directing all the fury of the westerlies straight down the Ross Glacier to Royal Bay on the east coast.

On South Georgia people learn to live with wind – even in Royal Bay. During the first international geophysical year, 1882–3, a German scientific expedition had lived here for several months and the inlet where we were based was named Moltke Harbour after the Germans' expedition ship, the first steam-powered vessel ever to reach South Georgia. Ninety-nine years later, the British Joint Services expedition landed by Nick Barker at Royal Bay made a comprehensive set of meteorological obser-vations for the summer months to compare with the Germans' records of a century earlier. Taken in conjunction with British Antarctic Survey records at King Edward Point, they indicate clearly a slight temperature rise since the nineteenth century, cor-roborated by glacial recession.

The Joint Services expeditioners also recorded higher mean wind speeds than the Germans and found the weather generally more stormy. They commented on the frequent abrupt changes in the weather and the localised nature of the funnelled katabatic winds. Like them, we made our base by the BAS hut about a quarter of a mile up from the shore in Whale Valley. Aligned north and south, the valley ought theoretically to have been well protected from the weather, but South Georgian wind seems to have a way of turning corners and coming at you from every direction. So, while the main force was crashing eastwards down the centre of Royal Bay, flanking divisions would sneak round the back of the mountains and come howling south down Whale Valley. During our second night there the big dome tent was pushed and pummelled out of shape. All night long, Lindsay and I were woken by damp fabric crushing down on our heads and by morning the poles were wildly distorted. Two days later the tent looked like a nasty compound fracture, with snapped poles punc-turing the skin at jagged angles. We patched it up and tried to improvise guy lines, which the manufacturers in their technological wisdom had failed to provide, but on the fourth day the whole edifice collapsed in a pile of ripped sodden fabric and mangled poles. Luckily we had a reserve tent, generously endowed with sturdy guy lines.

While suffering these domestic tribulations we started to shift supplies inland. The plan was to establish a secure base on the far side of the Ross Pass where we could eventually live for three weeks within range of our chosen peaks. First we made an immediate depot part-way up the Ross Glacier.

Julian, Brian and I set off on the first morning, finding a way around the headland to the inner bay of Little Moltke Harbour. It was an exciting moment as we traversed round the coast and got our first glimpse of the Ross Glacier front, misty blue under a damp blanket of cloud. As Duncan Carse had told us, there was an easy ramp from the beach up the side of the glacier but by now the Ross wind funnel was at work, trying to push us back down the ramp. With heads down we struggled doggedly to about 500 feet above sea level where we found a suitably prominent boulder for the depot. Braced with backs to the wind, we unpacked our rucksacks and left the first consignment of food and supplies under a great pile of stones, with a bundle of cane marker wands weighted against the boulder.

On the second day we were lazy. Five inches of snow lay on the ground, the wind was foul and our route round the cliffs was shrouded in mist so we stayed put, spending much of the day in the hut, working through several meals including an excellent loaf of bread baked by Kees. Julian entertained us with stories of the Eton Wall Game, revelling in memories of institutionalised violence, while Kees smiled at the tribal rituals of the English upper classes.

I had a bit of a cold the next morning and let the other four go without me, but on the fourth day I joined in the load-carry. Kees took a while getting organised and Lindsay had only just started on the day's first obligatory pint of tea when Julian, Brian and I set off. It was a bright sunny morning but as I walked round the headland and looked down across Royal Bay I could see great sheets of white spume charging over the turquoise. On the final climb to the depot I was blinded by a driving cloud of spindrift, stinging my eyes with ice particles and tearing the breath from my mouth. On the way back down, with the wind behind me, I almost took off.

Julian and Brian also reached the depot that day, but by the time Kees and Lindsay reached Little Moltke Harbour it was almost impossible to make headway into the wind. The sun was shining but they needed mittens and balaclavas to protect exposed skin from the vicious sand-blasting. Halfway across the beach they had to give up and turn round. I had my own problems climbing back round the headland. Several times the wind caught me off balance and knocked me to the ground and on one section, uncomfortably close to the cliff edge, I had to dash from boulder to boulder during lulls, clinging fearfully during each gust to stop the wind throwing me over the cliff.

The wind gave us a hard time but I enjoyed those journeys round the bay, getting to know the land and the animals and birds which lived there, so much better attuned than we to the wind, rain and snow. As well as the king penguins at Moltke Harbour, there was a colony of the smaller, dumpier gentoos a few hundred yards inland. As we set off in the morning across the springy turf of Whale Valley, the gentoos would usually be making their way down to the beach to join the kings for a day's fishing. We had to cross the river to gain the beach and a convocation of penguins would watch curiously as we waded through the icy current, either plunging straight in like Julian, or removing boots and socks in an attempt to do the whole day's work dry shod. Then round the beach, squeezing past a pod of sea elephant bulls heaving and belching indignantly at the disturbance. Further on there was another pod, mainly cows, wallowing in a foetid muddy hollow eroded between surviving clumps of tussock. Occasionally a fur seal would spring up from behind a boulder, growling with bared teeth. Sheathbills, little white scavengers with armour-plated beaks, scurried around like daft chickens and sometimes cormorants flew off from the rocks.

After half a mile cliffs barred the way and you had to climb high up wobbly steps of tussock. Halfway up the slope a small shelf of shorter, smoother grass was littered with old fish bones and penguin relics, and usually you would arrive to see the brown skua chick rushing to hide in a corner while its parents held up white-barred wings in defiance. At the last moment they would take off, circle wide, then swoop in fast, swerving clear at the last moment as you held up your protective ski stick. Apparently the northern skua, native to our Shetland Islands, sneaks up from behind, but this southern cousin attacks brazenly from the front, aiming straight for the intruder's eyes.

The crux of the route was a steep gully of loose earth and scree which you crossed very fast, looking nervously down at the big drop to the sea. Then more grass, high above the sea, with perhaps a light-mantled sooty albatross wheeling above the water, dancing straight-winged in the air like a super-elegant version of our own northern fulmars. Then a desert of earth and scree with reindeer tracks pointing the way to an easy slide to the beach. As you rushed down to Little Moltke Harbour you might see boulders of ice washed up on the beach, with sea elephants sleeping amongst them and the odd king or gentoo penguin strutting around. If there was a swarm of skrill offshore the penguins would be there, along with the little piebald Cape pigeons, flitting and darting in the surf.

Halfway round the beach you had to cross a meltwater stream, pushing off with ski sticks for a long hop and a jump. One day, Julian and I found three great elephants wedged in the stream, sleeping blissfully with heads half-submerged. Julian eyed up the animal bridge and looked at me with a provocative grin. 'I dare you!'

'But the poor things . . . it's cruel.'

'What? They wouldn't feel a thing with all that blubber.' He prodded one with his ski stick and I stood tentatively with one boot pressed into its hide. The animal snored on happily, so I stepped back to get momentum, then leapt forward and ran across the somnolent backs in three bounds. Only after Julian had followed did one of the bulls finally wake up, twist its head round and give us a token belch, before subsiding back into happy oblivion.

Sometimes, if a big bull felt threatened on a narrow stretch of beach, he would back off into the sea, rearing up on immensely powerful shoulders, baring dirty old molars and roaring defiant belches as he heaved his body backwards in great ripples of undulating blubber. This was how they had tried, in vain, to escape when the hunters used to come each summer for their quota of blubber. Duncan Carse had told us about the industry, speaking with some affection for the sealers who worked these beaches until the mid-Sixties. It was they, operating from the old whale-catchers *Diaz* and *Albatros*, now rotting at the Grytviken jetty, who had, in return for the odd bottle of whisky, put Carse ashore at Royal Bay and other beaches all around the island to set off on his exploratory journeys inland. The sealers were a tough, eccentric, polyglot bunch, many of them Argentinian Poles. They worked in dangerous conditions, rowing ashore in little prams, through a heaving swell, often contending with icebergs, rock reefs and oar-catching tentacles of kelp.

After landing, one oarsman would hold the pram ready just offshore while the rest of the crew worked the beach, selecting the biggest bulls for slaughter. Once a bull was selected, one man would drive it to the shore by tapping its sensitive proboscis with a long pole. Just as the bull reached the water's edge the marksman would shoot it with a single bullet through the head. Then the flensers set to with their knives, stripping the hide in a single piece with its great layer of blubber attached. It could weigh over a ton, and once it was toggled up with a rope looped through the flipper holes, it took several men to drag it into the water where it could be towed, floating, behind the waiting pram.

Duncan Carse recorded it all in a harrowing series of photographs. One of the most poignant shows a sealing vessel waiting offshore in a wide expanse of turquoise water, with snowy peaks behind. In the foreground a crowded little pram is struggling out between rock shoals, towing its shapeless bundle of blubber through churning surf scarlet with blood.

South Georgia's elephant seals, less valuable than the fur seals, survived the ravages of the nineteenth century and when sealing was resumed this century the population was quite stable; once the Falklands government started to enforce strict quotas its survival was guaranteed. In fact Nigel Bonner, who was the sealing inspector from 1956 to 1962, pointed out with characteristic detachment that controlled culling of bulls actually served to increase the population. Because of the harem system many bulls never get a chance to mate and the majority of them are, from a reproductive point of view, redundant. Five times as large as the cows, they also consume a disproportionate share of food in the surrounding ocean. With the elimination of surplus bulls, there was more food available for the cows, which grew faster and reproduced younger.

In contrast to the catastrophic depletion of whale stocks, the brutal harvest of elephant seals on South Georgia was successful in maintaining, even strengthening, a renewable resource. But it was only commercially viable on the back of the much bigger shore-based whaling operation, as elephant seal oil accounted for a small proportion of total production. For instance, during the 1960–1 season – the last big whale catch on South Georgia – 109,727 40-gallon barrels of whale oil were produced, as opposed to just 12,381 barrels of seal oil. The seal oil was a useful boost to profits, but once the infrastructure of the bigger industry collapsed, sealing had no future on its own.

So, after 1965, the elephant seals were left in peace and the South Georgia population has since stood at about 350,000. Arriving on the island in late December, we had missed the most exciting part of the seals' year. After a winter at sea, the bulls pull up on to the beaches in September, followed by the cows. Most of the cows give birth to a single pup in October, followed by three weeks' lactation. The pup grows incredibly fast and is soon independent, while the mother loses up to 40 per cent body-weight. Meanwhile the beach resounds with the bellowing and roaring of the bulls fighting furiously to guard their harems. Once the mother cows have finished breastfeeding they are rounded up for mating, but by that stage the cow is so weak that after mating she has to go back to sea and feed for two or three months before she is fit enough for the egg to be implanted in the uterus.

During our walks around Royal Bay we were only seeing a small fraction of the animals that would have been crowding the beaches earlier that spring. The bulls we saw sparring half-heartedly were probably either disappointed young studs who had failed to establish a harem or old men now past it, with only the furrowed scars on their immense necks to commemorate former glories. Most of the adults and now many of the pups were out at sea. In the winter they would all be gone for months, roaming the

Southern Ocean. It was sobering to think that the clumsy lumbering animals we saw on land had another whole life of mastery at sea, about which we knew virtually nothing. A good deal of mystery still surrounds the pelagic life of the elephant seal, but zoologists are starting to build up a picture. Two BAS men, Tom Arnbom and Alastair Taylor, had spent that spring working at Husvik and already had some interesting statistics about the elephant seal's life at sea.

As far as they could tell, the seals feed almost exclusively on squid and they calculate that the 350,000 animals on South Georgia consume about 2.7 million metric tons a year. They still don't know quite how far the seals roam, nor the exact location of the squid they catch, but in future satellite monitoring should make the picture clearer. However, Taylor and Arnbom, using simple radio transmitters, had already collected some amazing diving statistics, monitoring one tagged seal off South Georgia. In three and a half weeks it dived 1600 times, with an average duration of eighteen minutes and only two minutes' average breather between each dive. Even more extraordinary than this stamina was the depths to which it dived, on one occasion reaching 800 metres below the surface. When I expressed astonishment at mammals being able to withstand the colossal pressures at those depths, Tom explained that the seals have a special mechanism of elastic blood vessels in their ears; apparently Australian zoologists based on McQuarrie Island have recorded an elephant seal diving to 1500 metres!

We were walking along the beach one morning when we noticed a seal lying all alone. Then as we drew closer we realised that its fur was paler, greyer and more mottled than usual, and that its body seemed elongated, with a strange-shaped head. As soon as it turned to show its wide slit of a mouth, we realised it was a leopard seal. We stared for a while at its powerful flippers, serpent's head and that horribly smiling mouth, but it virtually ignored us. Then, feeling guiltily like some molesting child, determined to make the animal react for the camera, I threw a small stone at the seal's side. It responded immediately, flicking up its head and gaping open its mouth to reveal two vicious rows of triple-barbed teeth.

The leopard seal occasionally feeds on other seals but its main prey is the penguin. On land the penguins have little to fear but the leopard hunts them in water, often hiding amongst the kelp, waiting to snatch a passing bird and skin it with one toss of its fanged head. There is no record of a leopard seal ever attacking a man but they are renowned for inquisitiveness, often swimming close to small boats. They could presumably topple a small dinghy and a few snaps of those powerful jaws would make quick work of a human; so it is understandable that the whalers, who had no fine feelings for Antarctic wildlife, nearly always shot the animals when they saw them. Even on the beach, where the leopard seal is virtually immobile, we kept a respectful distance. A few weeks later, stumbling at nightfall round the shore of Cumberland East Bay, Brian almost trod on a leopard seal and gave himself quite a fright. He moved out of the way very quickly.

When we saw that first leopard seal at Little Moltke Harbour, we were finally on our way up into the mountains. After five days load-carrying round the bay, the time had come to move up and make our base near the Ross Pass. We had assumed all along that lightweight tents would be of only limited use on South Georgia and, now that one tent had already been destroyed, we were even keener on the idea of excavating a snowcave to make a secure base in the mountains. So on December 23rd the four climbers set off heavily laden to start digging. Once we found a suitable site, Brian and Lindsay would be left with food supplies for a few days to construct a cave, while Julian and I returned to Royal Bay to continue load-carrying round the bay.

For the first time on the trip we roped up, now that we were moving up the main glacier with its hundreds of crevasses concealed under snow. We also wore snowshoes to spread our weight on the soft surface and take some of the drudgery out of trail-breaking.

Ropes, harnesses, snowshoes, suncream, sunglasses . . . all the paraphernalia of glacier travel which I hadn't used for months. And real mountains with glinting icefields, blue-green séracs, sweeping snowfields and ridges encrusted with towers of icing sugar. It was good to be back again and for several hours I plodded happily, carving our track up the wide expanse of glacier. But as we approached the pass I began to flag a little. Brian and Lindsay were now ahead, pushing effortlessly up into the clouds that seemed to clog the pass perpetually. I followed on another rope with Julian, who had gone very quiet apart from the occasional protest such as, 'I'm going to have to go down soon. I've had enough.'

Brian had spent most of the previous year roaming the Outer Hebrides, collecting air samples for his research. Lindsay had been on three Himalayan expeditions during the last twelve months and was also very fit. They showed no sign of stopping, not even when we reached the great flat sweep of the pass.

'For God's sake, stop and wait for a moment,' I yelled. They waited for us, to discuss plans. 'Carse said the best campsite was under the ridge of nunataks.'

'You mean this lot here, dividing the Brögger and Spenceley glaciers?' Brian had out the map and was pointing to the spot heights of little rock outcrops known in the trade as nunataks. We had now crossed the watershed and were on the Brögger Glacier. Julian looked morose. I felt tired and had no desire to walk another mile to Carse's campsite.

Clutching lazily at straws, I suggested stopping where we were. 'How about digging a temporary hole here and rigging up the remains of the tent in it?'

Lindsay laughed scornfully, 'I'm not sure that's a very good idea.'

'You could find somewhere better in the morning and dig – '

'Don't be bloody crazy!' Brian interrupted. 'Do you really think we're going to stop right here, with no proper shelter, in the middle of the worst wind funnel on the whole island?'

'Yes, I suppose you're right, but the further we walk beyond the pass the longer the journeys are going to be when it comes to ferrying stuff up from the depot.'

'All right, just give us half an hour and I'll find a windscoop.' Brian had often enthused on the subject of windscoops, recalling fondly the huge ones he had seen on the Antarctic Peninsula, formed by the wind blasting across a flat expanse of snow, crashing into rock cliffs and deflecting sideways to carve a great hollow from the snow's edge. He was convinced that if we cut back to the cliffs enclosing the Ross Pass, we ought to find a good scoop on this windward side. So, directing from behind, Julian and I sent the other two off on a revised compass bearing and the caravan moved off through the cloud.

Ten minutes later, dead on target, we found ourselves walking along a slight crest with vertical snow walls dropping away to our left. Then the mist parted a little to reveal the dark shapes of a rock castle separated from us by a seventy-feet-deep moat. We followed the crest round for another hundred yards or so until the angle of the snow wall eased, allowing us to run and slide down to the bottom of the moat.

We had left the hut at 7.30 that morning and it was now 5.30 p.m. Julian and I had a long walk back down and it would be dark in four and a half hours. We stopped to melt snow for a restorative cup of tea then set off, leaving the other two with supplies for a few days. Looking back at them, starting to excavate a cave in the wall of the scoop, we marvelled at this wonderful secret valley tucked under the wide expanse of glacier. Then, as we emerged from the valley, South Georgia treated us to one of its most magical, theatrical transformation scenes.

The mist thinned and the light brightened from dull grey to sparkling silver. The rock castle behind us grew close and solid and the snow underfoot took form. Above the northern rim of the scoop white towers appeared in the sky. At first they were apparitions without scale; then, as we reached the rim of the scoop, the mist rolled right away to reveal the whole expanse of the Ross Pass and Brögger Glacier.

Julian pleaded, 'Can we just have two minutes to look at all this – we might never see it again?' So we stopped to absorb it all, forgetting the afternoon's drudgery of load-carrying in this first magical vision of the island's west coast, a shimmering haze of ice, water and sky, where the Brögger Glacier flowed out into the sea. The sky to the north was now quite clear, and we picked out the Allardyce peaks against the deep blue.

'That must be Nordenskjöld.'

'Yes – with that huge ice face . . . and Kling tucked in to the right – '

'And Roots behind it – with a long flat summit . . . and that huge mass behind must be Paget.'

'What about these near ones?'

'Just across the pass?'

'Yes, on this ridge descending from Brooker. Lovely peaks. I bet they haven't been climbed.'

'And they're only an hour from the scoop.'

We planted a marker wand on the rim of the scoop, took a compass bearing from the edge of the Ross Pass to make sure we could find it on future whiteout journeys, then started down in high spirits. We raced the twelve-mile return to Moltke Harbour, pausing only occasionally to savour the most beautiful evening so far on the island. Nevertheless, the darkness beat us and the final traverse round the tussock cliffs was a stumbling affair as the two clumsy humans thrashed their way past unseen protesters, belching, squawking and trumpeting in the night.

On the final home beach two gigantic elephant bulls ignored our torchbeams, intent on their private vendetta, lifting their heads high to crash down, one jaw thudding noisily on the other's neck. We raced on across the beach, through the river and up Whale Valley, finally arriving at 11 p.m. to find the hut immaculately cleaned and tidied by Kees, who plied us with soup, cheese, potato, mince and pints of apple juice. At midnight I got into my sleeping bag and five minutes later I was asleep.

On Christmas Eve we had visitors. Luckily we were in, having decided to take a rest, after the previous day's long haul to the Ross Pass and back. It was a gorgeous balmy afternoon and for once we were spared the nerve-racking hammer of the wind. The only sound was the background blur of sea, waterfall and animal noises. Then it was broken by the unmistakable clatter of a helicopter engine. One of the pilots on the *Endurance* had promised that he might drop in and see us that week, if he had time on the way to or from supplying the Royal Engineers doing survey work at Cape Charlotte, over the bay. He might even take some of our gear up on to the Ross Glacier.

The noise grew louder and we suddenly spotted the Lynx's red markings high above the valley. Two minutes later it landed and we rushed over, ducking beneath the blades. The pilot kept his engine running as he shouted above the din, 'I'm in a hurry – just dropped in to see how you are.'

'Not time to do a depot then?' I shouted, disappointed.

The pilot hesitated for a moment, allowing Julian to stick his head into the cockpit and plead, 'Couldn't you just do a quick journey up on to the glacier?'

'All right, but it'll have to be quick and I can't take those barrels. I'll be back in five minutes.'

The helicopter roared off around the headland and we rushed over to the barrels, throwing all the remaining food and gear destined for the glacier depot into plastic fertiliser bags. When the helicopter returned we heaved them up to the flight observer, Ian, along with the hefty bundle of skis and marker wands. I also threw in two bottles of Famous Grouse and the letter I had written to Rosie in hopeful anticipation of this visit. 'Please will you post it? Happy Christmas!'

Julian, with true leaderly initiative, had grabbed some emergency warm clothes and climbed into the cockpit to guide the pilot to our depot. Luckily the emergency clothes were not needed and ten minutes later the helicopter deposited him back at the hut, looking very pleased with himself. 'It's all up near the Ross Pass.'

'What?' The pilot had agreed just to take the remaining supplies up to our depot near the snout of the glacier. But, pushing his luck, Julian had suggested collecting the existing depot and moving the whole lot up to the Ross Pass. The brazen begging worked, for the good-natured pilot agreed to fly as high as he could. The Ross Pass itself was under cloud, but by the time they reached the cloud ceiling they were most of the way up the glacier.

Julian got out the map to show where they had landed. 'Just here, on the south side of the glacier, by this prominent rock ridge. The wind up there is hideous – it must be the worst place on the whole glacier – really dangerous! He had to land on a slope, with just one wheel touching, pointing it into the wind ... really struggling to keep it in control. Ian just threw the stuff out of the door and didn't let me put up a marker. The skis – you know how heavy that bundle is? – well they just flew threw the air, pulled out of my hands. Anyway, I piled rocks on the whole lot and then they made me get back in the chopper. Tidy bit of work, eh?'

In just five minutes our kind friends from the *Endurance* had saved us at least a week's tedious load-carrying, making a mockery of our previous efforts. We could not have asked for a better Christmas present. I suggested that we celebrated by breaking into our one box of Cabernet Sauvignon, part of the essential groceries donated by Marks & Spencer. Lindsay and Brian would miss out but, after all, it was Christmas Eve.

'Yes,' Kees concurred, 'it is a good occasion. But any occasion is a good occasion. In any case, they wouldn't appreciate it.'

They probably would have appreciated it, but Brian in particular seemed much less hedonistic than some of us. Modern British expeditions tend to suffer from brutally functional catering and Kees noted with approval that, instead of the endless rice and dahl he had been force-fed in Nepal, he was now treated to stuffed eggs and caviar, salami, olives and artichoke hearts. Julian also professed high standards, but chauvinism got the better of him when we commented on the prevailing awfulness of English institutional food. 'I don't agree. I've eaten just as bad food on the Continent.'

'But I have travelled very widely in Europe,' Kees insisted, 'and there's nothing to equal bad English food.'

'I've travelled a lot, too. English food can be terrible, I agree, but it can be just as bad on the Continent.'

'Well, you have to search very hard to find it,' Kees concluded quietly, reaching for his cigars. The insignificant Euro-squabble was just part of the undercurrent of subtle tensions that seem an essential part of expedition life; and, as if to mock the pettiness of our sparrings, the short-wave radio brought us crackling news, that Christmas, of momentous events 8000 miles away. There was something quite bizarre about sitting in that little hut, isolated from the rest of the world, with only the crackling bulletins from the BBC World Service to tell us about the great revolution in Eastern Europe. History was being made while we sipped wine amongst the seals and penguins, cut off from it all. But it was Christmas, with its associations of home and tradition, that really heightened our isolation.

Julian, in particular, was feeling homesick, and seemed increasingly moody although he managed to rise to the occasion when we spotted the Antarctic cruise ship, *Society Explorer*, steaming across Royal Bay, shouting 'Tourists!' in mock derision. It was Christmas morning, an incomparably beautiful morning, and we were on our way up to the Ross Glacier to secure and mark the helicopter depot. We dallied in Moltke Harbour, repeating sections of the route for Kees to film. Wading barefoot through the river was a tingling delight, the sea sparkled, the air was warm, it was midsummer and I had hardly ever experienced a better day in the wilds. Up on the glacier a gentle föhn wind was blowing, absurdly warm, melting depressions in the snow surface to turquoise pools.

Julian led us to the depot, where we secured all the supplies under huge boulders and erected marker wands, then we returned down the glacier. I have never seen colour like it: ice, snow, sea and sky shimmering in streaks of sapphire, turquoise and violet; and as we returned home round the cliffs and made our way back up the beach, dawdling amongst the penguins, I felt at last that this was where I really wanted to be. Back at base, still in the same contented mood, I had just finished washing in the stream and was 'changing for dinner' when Julian called me over to his tent. 'Can I have a word with you?'

I went over to his tent and asked what it was. He looked rather embarrassed. 'There's something I need to talk about.'

'Okay. Hang on and I'll get the tobacco.' I also fetched two mugs of whisky for good measure, then, as we sat in the evening sunshine rolling our cigarettes, he explained.

'I've just been unwrapping some presents from Elaine . . . it must be Christmas . . . I don't know . . . anyway, I've been missing her terribly, feeling homesick – '

'It's quite normal.'

'Yes, maybe, but I don't feel happy about the mountains. It just doesn't feel right. It's never happened before, in the Alps or in Africa, but I feel nervous about climbing.'

So that was why he had been so quiet. I thought of all the times I had been to the mountains, hated them and wished that I could break a leg and have the excuse to go home. Twice I had arrived in the Alps in midwinter to announce to my companion that actually I did not want to climb – the mountains had suddenly become

hateful, frightening things. On both occasions, with a little prod-
ding, I had managed to regain confidence. Nowadays I seemed to
be able to cope better, knowing what to expect, but Julian had
only been climbing a short while and had less experience than the
rest of us of going away on prolonged expeditions.

I said something along those lines, probably sounding desperately patronising, but by the time Julian had talked with Kees as
well, and we had all had more drink, eaten a good meal and
opened some Christmas presents, he seemed a lot more cheerful.
We assured him that there was no pressure on him to climb
anything, although he might as well help get the snowcave base
established and see how he felt after a few days at the Ross Pass.

On Boxing Day Julian moved into the bigger tent with me, as his
smaller one was to be taken up to the Ross Pass. I spent most of
the day in bed, reading my Christmas present from Rosie, Julian
Barnes' *History of the World in 10½ Chapters*. The black
humour, the dismal view of mankind and the recurring shipwreck
theme were matched by conditions outside the tent. It did not rain
in Whale Valley, but we saw big clouds race in from the west, torn
grey and smudged at the edges as they shed their load up in the
mountains. Huge waves of spume silvered the turquoise bay and
twenty-foot-high clouds of dirty yellow sand blasted across the
beach. Later we heard that at King Edward Point the anemometer
went off the scale. They estimated gusts of 140 knots – probably a
slight exaggeration, but the wind was certainly wild that day. We
would laugh nervously as each gust announced itself with a scream
up the valley. Then it would rush down and across to explode with
a loud bang on the ridge above. The tent – the Super Nova which
had replaced the first disaster – survived, but only by dint of
whipping and flexing in the gusts.

That night we heard that Samuel Beckett had just died in Paris,
the Americans had invaded Panama and President Ceauşescu and
his wife had been executed by firing squad in Romania.

There was still no rain on the 27th and less wind, so Kees and I
carried round the final odds and ends that missed the helicopter to
the lower glacier depot. The wind was quite fierce at the depot and
the glacier above was obliterated by cloud, but it was only late in
the evening that we heard what conditions had really been like up

at the Ross Pass. I was just settling down in bed, Walkman switched on, plugged into Puccini, when there was a noise of footsteps and voices outside. Unsociable and reluctant to stir, I let Julian go out to meet Lindsay and Brian. A few minutes later he came back to the tent and announced melodramatically, 'There's a lake in the windscoop. The snowcave's under water.'

In the hut Lindsay and Brian repeated the story for my benefit. They were surrounded by a great pile of sodden clothes and they both looked exhausted. Lindsay explained how it had got warmer and warmer, with the föhn wind, on Christmas Day. 'Everything was just dripping; it was horrendous!'

'But couldn't you pitch the tent inside?'

'Ah, the tent!' he shouted triumphantly. 'The tent! I think we would have been marginally better off without it.'

On Boxing Day they, like us, had experienced hurricane winds; on the Ross Pass there had also been precipitation. 'But it wasn't snow: it was raining – right up there, at 2000 feet. Everything was just soaked. Then this morning I poked me 'ead out of the door, had a look, and turned round to Brian and said, "Hey, Brian, me old fruitcake,"' and his eyes lit up at the memory of it, '"there's a lake out here."'

After all that warmth and rain and wind, everything had melted and percolated through to fill up the bottom of our secret valley. By the time Lindsay and Brian had packed up to leave, the water was lapping at the front door. They stowed all the gear on some rocks well above the high tide mark and left, taking all day to thrash their way down on compass bearings through the blizzard.

Three days' hard work and all we had to show for it was a decaying submerged snowcave. We seemed to have lost round one at the Ross Pass. Now there was nothing for it but to go up and start all over again.

8

The Ice Palace

Christmas was celebrated officially on December 28th. Lindsay had a stocking-full of presents from Jan, including a giant book of crosswords intended to while away stormy days in the snowcave, when it was finally built. Julian provided crackers and Elaine's presents, there was a stocking from my parents and Brian, in complete secrecy, had brought each of us a beautifully appropriate book. For Lindsay, the survivor of countless epics, he had chosen Apsley Cherry-Garrard's version of Scott's last expedition, *The Worst Journey in the World*; for Kees, the photographer Ponting's account, *The Great White South*, and, for Julian, Evans' *South with Scott*. As Everest Hero, I had something slightly different, inscribed 'To Stephen, who "has been higher than most"' – the hilarious fictional account of the world's highest peak, 40,000½ feet above sea level, *The Ascent of Rum Doodle*.

Two months earlier, packing all the supply barrels in Shropshire, we had taken heed of the old adage that 'any old fool can be uncomfortable'. Freighting gear out by sea, with no strict weight limit, had allowed us to make the most of Marks & Spencer's sponsorship and cater for an adequate Christmas dinner. The first course was our now well-rehearsed formula of stuffed eggs with caviar, Parma ham, artichoke hearts and olives, washed down with a couple of bottles of Champagne chilled on fragments of iceberg. We moved on to red wine with the main course of Fortnum's goose quenelles, mashed potato, French beans and asparagus. In the absence of brandy, whisky butter was a more than adequate accompaniment to a dark, rich, vaporous Christmas pudding; and, to end on a suitably mellow note, Kees produced his finest cigars to go with the Port.

There was still, though, the little matter of our snowcave. Brian was keen to get back up to the Ross Pass as soon as possible and start work on a new base. Once again he observed that it was pointless for us all to go up immediately; much better to stagger our arrival until a reasonable-sized cave was ready. I was keen to do some digging so I volunteered to go up ahead with him.

First we had to wait another day. The weather had deteriorated on the 28th and the next day there was heavy rain and sleet from dawn to dusk. I emerged only twice from the tent: once to collect breakfast from the hut staff and a second time, nine hours later, to get supper. But on the 30th there was an improvement, so Brian and I set off in the evening. The others came down to the beach to say goodbye as we waded the river and headed off round the coast.

We planned to spend at least three weeks up in the interior of the island and I felt a little sad crossing the twilit beach of Little Moltke Harbour, saying goodbye to the sea elephants. But there was also the familiar excitement of starting off on a mountain journey, climbing steadily up the glacier in the cool of the night when the snow was, more or less, firmly frozen underfoot. It was a beautiful night with a yellow moon half-veiled by clouds and a bright green star, perhaps Venus, in the north-east, prompting Brian to one of his rare moments of half-uttered romanticism. We stopped to rest for five minutes every hour, but otherwise plodded in silence. Alone on that dark field of snow, I thought about Rosie, nearly 8000 miles away in the Alps. I had no way of knowing that she was bored and depressed, stuck in France on minimal pay for a disastrous, snowless winter with a dreary succession of disappointed clients to placate. Instead I fondly imagined the cosy chiaroscuro of some warm chalet or bar, with moonlit snow outside, and rather wished that I was there.

We were quicker this time, reaching the windscoop in just seven and a half hours from the hut. We had brought up Julian's excellent little two-man tent to pitch as a temporary shelter on the side of the scoop and by 4 a.m. on New Year's Eve we were both ensconced for a few hours' sleep. But the others were due later that day, so at 9 o'clock we got up to start work.

There was no trace of the old snowcave and a huge lake, frozen green, filled the bottom of our secret valley. This time we were taking no chances and I made the first incision far above high tide level, only twelve feet below the level of the glacier plateau. This was going to be the best, biggest snowcave in Antarctica and no effort was spared. First we excavated the front door, digging deep into the side of the scoop, taking care to keep the aperture as small as possible because we would need to shut it during blizzards. We took half-hour turns, hacking out large blocks of compacted snow and tumbling them down the slope on to the frozen lake. Once the entrance tunnel was bored eight feet into the scoop wall, we could start to enlarge the interior, burrowing sideways to enlarge the main chamber until there was room for both of us to work.

Finesse is not the word that springs to mind when I recall Brian. On a superficial level he looks a mess, with a unique collection of weathered rags dating from his days with the British Antarctic Survey. But it is the actual body language that is most uncouth. Of course he is masterly on steep rock and ice, but on flat ground he goes to pieces, limbs flying wildly in every direction, apparently incapable of moving in a straight line. When it came to mining, the man from County Durham seemed to have no method at all, throwing himself at the coalface with flailing arms, hacking indis-criminately.

I preferred to slice methodically, scoring a grid of one-foot squares with the snow saw, then prising out neat cubes with the shovel. Brian said it was the carpenter in me and I told him about my spell working for a mutual climbing friend who is a furniture maker. There seem to be a lot of climbers who work with wood, but Luke Hughes is an unusually good designer. When I men-tioned this Brian replied, 'I wouldn't know what a good design is. I mean, a table is just something you sit at for writing and eating.'

'Ah, but if it is well designed, you will write better and eat better, and have the pleasure of something beautiful.' For the moment though, the finer points of design at the Ross Pass had to wait. The overall plan was slowly taking shape but the urgent task was just to create a big enough chamber for the other three to sleep in that night. We worked hard, hacking, slicing, shovelling and pushing through the day, oblivious of the wind and sleet outside. By the time the others arrived that evening there was a large pile of blocks on the frozen lake; inside there was room for all three to spread out their insulating mats and sleeping bags in the main chamber.

Brian and I retreated to the tent on the far side of the scoop, where I had secreted a tipple of whisky for a token New Year's Eve celebration. We ought really to have shared it with the others but there was only a small sip left and we were so warmly settled in our sleeping bags . . .

We started the new decade with a late breakfast. Then, after a cramped struggle back into damp clothes and sodden boots, we went across to join the others at the coalface. Julian, who had built his own house extension in Shropshire, proved the master builder, or rather excavator, discovering that the snow saw achieved best results with rapid downward strokes, scoring deep grooves in the snow. He had also had the foresight to bring up an old steel spade from Royal Bay, which stood up much better than our light alloy snow shovels to the rigours of levering out the blocks. Two people would work at the face, while the other three handed back the blocks to be flung out of the door.

The weather was foul that day, with fresh snow swirling around the entrance. Because it was so foul we urged Kees to do some filming, recording what it was really like making our mountain home. Reluctantly he unpacked the precious Aaton and did his best to wipe off the all-pervasive snow and dampness. But it was the shortest take in cinema history, for after only a few seconds the camera seized up. Ten days were to pass before it would work again.

By evening the main chamber was complete. It ran north from the entrance, parallel with the scoop wall, and was ten feet long by eight feet wide with headroom for even Lindsay to stand up. In Pakistan once I had slept in a hastily dug shallow snowcave, cowering claustrophobically beneath a slowly sagging roof. But this construction was in a different league. The outside wall was at least six feet thick and ten feet of hard-packed snow lay between the ceiling and the plateau above. The final sophistication was to suspend the pale yellow remains of the big dome tent inside the chamber, creating an effect rather like a wedding marquee. Unfortunately it was not a complete success and in the days to come we chided ourselves for not bringing up the third tent. The improvised

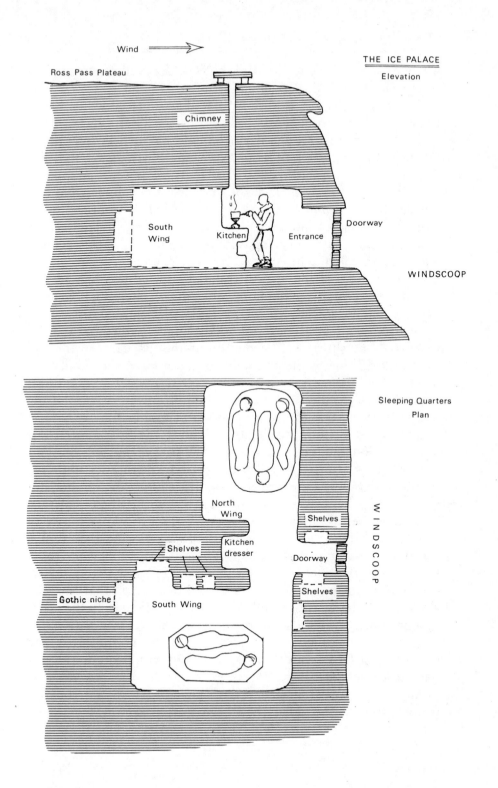

Wind ⟹

Ross Pass Plateau

THE ICE PALACE
Elevation

Chimney

South
Wing   Kitchen   Entrance

Doorway

WINDSCOOP

Sleeping Quarters
Plan

North
Wing

Shelves

Kitchen
dresser

Doorway

Shelves

Shelves

Gothic niche   South Wing

WINDSCOOP

marquee kept off the worst drips, but it never really combated the APD syndrome – All Pervading Damp.

The wind relented a little on January 2nd, allowing Brian, Lindsay and me to go for a walk down the Ross Glacier, navigating by compass through a clinging mist to the helicopter depot to collect the first batch of food and two pairs of skis. On the third the weather was beautiful, so Brian and I made the final journey right down to the original depot to collect the supplies that had missed the helicopter carry. Skis transformed the journey into a glorious skimming glide over the surface. It put me in an excellent mood so that I forgave Brian his infuriating misuse of skis, scrawling random, inefficient, unaesthetic scribbles across the glacier instead of the straight, logical tramlines for which they are designed. I even forgave him his enviable fitness, charging bludgeon-like back up the glacier, leaving me far behind with no foreground for my photos. Instead of trying to keep up I stopped to say hello to two skuas sitting in the middle of the glacier, content and satiated, with the feathery remains of an ill-fated sheathbill scattered around them on the snow. I had no idea why they had flown up the glacier with their carrion, but they were a comforting reminder of the seaside life we had left behind us.

After a rest I continued the long climb to the Ross Pass. It was late afternoon and the snow was wet and sticky, clogging my skins – the strips of artificial fur, like sealskin, which you stick to the ski soles for climbing, allowing the skis to slide forwards but not backwards. It was tedious work but the reward, when I emerged into the westering sun at the Ross Pass, was a magical expanse of shimmering silver. Even up here, perhaps enjoying the evening sunshine, another bird, dark, almost black, with a tiny white rump patch and forked tail like a martin, was skimming incongruously over the glistening snow desert. Later I discovered that this tiny sky gypsy is the world's smallest seabird – a member of the petrel family which also includes the largest seabird, the wandering albatross. It is called the Wilson's petrel, after the artist and ornithologist Dr Edward Wilson, who died with Scott on the way back from the Pole.

After that magical finish to a day's skiing I returned to the cave in high spirits. The others had been busy and now the second chamber was complete, running south-west from the doorway and separated from the original chamber by a huge pillar, into which the kitchen dresser was set. The smaller, better tent was now pitched in the new wing and Julian had laid out his and my gear, leaving Brian to join the lower ranks in the damp marquee in the north wing. We seemed to be repeating the unfair cabin arrangements on the *Endurance* and I felt a little uneasy about hogging the more comfortable bedroom – but not uneasy enough to do anything about it. Perhaps, if we had been more democratic and rotated places, we could have diffused the little tensions in the group. Instead they exploded the next afternoon.

It should have been a perfect day. Kees and I had the cave to ourselves while the others did a load-carry from the helicopter depot. Now that supplies were building up in the cave I spent the morning constructing storage space, carving cupboards into the walls of the south wing, embellishing them with pilasters and a large Romanesque column. On the back wall I went for mature Gothic, carving a large niche framed in a delicate ogee arch. The Aaton was still on strike so Kees used the standby video camera to record the artisan at work. Then we completed the housework, sorting out all the gas cylinders and groceries, stacking them on the various larder shelves and enlarging the kitchen dresser in the entrance lobby.

The others returned at tea-time to destroy this scene of domestic contentment by suggesting that we should actually go climbing. I was so intent on getting our base completely stocked that I had rather forgotten about climbing mountains. Of course the weather did, as Brian observed, look promising, but his particular wording was the problem. 'I think I'll wander up and have a look at that ridge towards Vogel Peak.'

Julian and I exploded simultaneously. 'What do you mean, "I"? What about the rest of us? I thought this was meant to be a team effort!'

'Well, I just fancied a wander. You can do what you like.'

'But for God's sake, can't we have a plan?' Julian groaned. He had worked off his Christmas doubts and fears, but there was still an edginess. Over the last year he had put a lot of work into organising the trip and he wanted some say in what we climbed and how we climbed it. I felt the same, and if Kees was to have any chance of making a coherent film, we needed some degree of coordination.

Lindsay remained non-committal, absorbed in his mug of tea, while I muttered angrily about 'typical bloody British expeditions – everyone rushing off in different directions and getting nowhere'. Brian reluctantly got out the map for a team discussion. We had been keen all along to attempt Vogel Peak and Brian, in particular, had been struck by its imposing pyramid as we made our way up the Ross Glacier. This was the view which had inspired the German expedition of 1881–2 to call it the 'Matterhorn Peak'. The Antarctic Place Names Committee later insisted on the more prosaic Vogel Peak, after the German expedition glaciologist, but whatever its name it remained a fine mountain, still unclimbed. The steep North Face was tempting but there was probably a more feasible route up the back, from this western side of the Ross Pass. Brian had spotted a ridge immediately behind the windscoop which might lead on to Vogel. I was sceptical, but he suggested that we could at least reach one of the subsidiary rocky pinnacles on the ridge, getting a minor summit in the bag and finding more about the lie of the land in the process.

So the five of us set off in a spirit of reluctant camaraderie. Within minutes South Georgia transcended our petty squabbles, treating us to another of its magical transformation scenes as we climbed up the glacier above the Ross Pass cloud bank. A golden light began to glow through the mist, dim shapes materialised into mountains and we emerged into brightness. Brian and Lindsay seemed hell bent on reaching our ridge but Kees, Julian and I, on the second rope, kept stopping to stare and photograph and shout our joy to the world as we wandered round in awestruck circles, tripping over the rope. Julian was a happy man again, seeing for the first time a magnificent jungle of mountains to the south, emerging in tangled confusion from fiery sunset clouds.

Somewhere in that confusion lay the Spenceley Glacier, the route we would take if we ever managed to travel south to Mt Carse, but for the moment it was enough just to be out on this beautiful evening. Back to the north the peaks of the Allardyce Range, dominated by the distant bulk of Mt Paget, were briefly peach-coloured before fading to a pale violet, then white, then grey. It was almost dark by the time we reached the crest of our ridge. A deep trough separated us from Vogel Peak but, invoking a well-worn cliché, we agreed that 'time spent in reconnaissance is never wasted'.

Brian and Lindsay rushed on, like two dogs set free, determined to find the highest of several identical insignificant bumps on the ridge. We set off back down to get supper heated. Reversing the steep ice slope we had just climbed, I protected Kees with the rope as he was not very familiar with crampons, the boot spikes which can catch so easily on a trouser leg and send you plummeting head over heels. Then the slope eased off and we reverted to snowshoes for the final plod back to the windscoop. Now that it was completely dark we also wore headtorches, anxious not to lose the tracks leading back home. Then the cloud welled up again from the Ross Pass, reflecting our headlights with blank whiteness, so we had to go dipped, lowering our beams to the ground to pick out the faint footsteps. It was an eerie sensation, moving three in line through the silent featureless fog, descending the hidden folds of the glacier until the welcoming marker wands appeared at the edge of the scoop. There we turned right, down a few steps to a slight platform, then stooped to walk through the front door, straight into the kitchen where we finally took off the rope.

By the time Lindsay and Brian returned the pasta was heated and it was a fairly contented team that sat down to supper. Prompted by Brian, we had done our first climbing on South Georgia, experienced an utterly memorable sunset, seen new vistas and got some valuable exercise, which was just as well, for that night another depression swept up the Brögger Glacier from the west.

For the next seven days we remained incarcerated in the ice palace.

9

The Blizzing Scale

We were, in fact, allowed out occasionally. One morning conditions were good enough for us to collect the remaining supplies from the helicopter depot and on two other occasions we emerged very briefly to take the air; but the rest of that week was spent locked up in the grotto.

I rather liked the predictable routine. At about eight in the morning I would wake gently to the blue twilight of another day. Kees was usually up first and would deliver tea and biscuits to the north and south wings, glancing disdainfully at the full pee bottles lined up outside each tent. Later he would bring porridge, strong coffee and, if we had recently baked a loaf, bread and honey. Lindsay would rise for his morning constitutional, walking five yards from the bedroom in the north wing, through the kitchen to the south wing, to settle like some medieval mystic in the Gothic niche, hunched over his mug of tea, gazing vacantly into the middle distance.

Later someone would have a look outside. If he did not yet need to leave the cave to relieve himself, the front door could be kept intact. All he need do was poke a small hole through the door with an ice axe shaft. With any luck a blast of fine spindrift through the hole would confirm blizzard conditions outside and we could all look forward to another day in bed.

We read a lot of books – an epic about the French Resistance, Dickens, Primo Levi, Cherry-Garrard's polar epic, a sad, beautiful novel by Paul Bailey, Kees's treasured copy of *A Far Off Place* and, as an antidote to Van der Post's high-minded seriousness, Donleavy's *Are You Listening, Rabbi Low?*, which had Julian and me laughing painfully at the ribald, lecherous anti-hero, Schultz.

Occasionally I emerged from these borrowed worlds of fantasy and imagination to ponder the banality of our own situation – five people lying day after day in a hole in the snow, achieving nothing, creating nothing – but mostly I relished the rare opportunity for undisturbed reading.

Once or twice a day I would get up for a little walk round the cave, perhaps taking the opportunity to cook a meal or prepare the dough for another loaf. Most of us shared domestic chores, although Julian was rarely seen washing dishes. Quoting Rosie, I explained to Kees, 'He thinks that little leprechauns come in the night to clear everything up.'

'No, he doesn't,' corrected Kees, 'he thinks that other people do it.'

Julian still lived in an ideal P. G. Wodehouse world where domestic trivia were dealt with by invisible menials but, for all its unreality, there was something touching about his reminiscences of Lafite-swilling evenings in Scotland, descriptions of Edwardian country house breakfasts and plans for his own modest cottage, where he hoped eventually to have rare breeds of chickens clucking in rural contentment and pigs worthy of Blandings Castle rooting about under the apple trees, completing a vision of Arcadian perfection.

It always seems to be the same on expeditions – the endless yearning for something different. One morning at breakfast, feeling a little homesick, I formulated a plan to visit Rosie for dinner that evening in the French Alps, 8000 miles away. I would have to have started at dawn and, given the foul weather, I would have to race on skis down the Ross Glacier to a point below the cloud ceiling where a helicopter would land and fly me to an aircraft carrier lying offshore. I would transfer immediately to a Harrier jump jet for a rapid flight to the Falklands, possibly requiring mid-flight refuelling from a Hercules. A specially chartered Concorde would be waiting at Mount Pleasant to fly me with supersonic urgency to Geneva, with refuelling at Ascension Island. From Geneva Airport it would only be a short hop by helicopter to Montchavin where Rosie would be waiting with a candlelit dinner.

The plan depended on perfect timing and the full cooperation of the Royal Navy, the RAF and British Airways, but it ought to be quite possible to reach Rosie in about ten hours from the snow-cave. I imagined that it would cost about £2 million. However, the biggest problem was put by Julian: 'Would you really feel like returning to the snowcave the next morning?'

That conversation took place on Monday, January 8th. Four days had passed since our evening excursion on the glaciers, and we had only been out briefly, on Sunday, to collect the remaining supplies from Helicopter Depot. On Tuesday I recorded in my diary:

> Storm continues. Wind rising in afternoon so that its howl is audible from inside. Mild feeling of incarceration, having not left the cave for two days. Only glimpse of the outside world has been a tiny chink of swirling brightness at the top of the door. Lindsay announces that the barometer is slowly rising. Perhaps the storm is starting to 'blow itself out'.

However, on Wednesday morning there was manic laughter from the north wing as Lindsay announced that his barometer had plummeted to a new low. But South Georgian weather defied the barometer and the weather actually improved slightly that day, allowing us to keep the front door open. After supper three of us went out to the plateau to enjoy the green-violet luminosity of dusk. Some of the lower summits were visible and we could just see down the Brögger Glacier to the ocean, apparently calm under a dark cloud stratum. It was so beautiful that we started to make plans for a climb the next morning, but as we descended the steps to the cave, Julian stuck his head out of the door to announce, 'Do you realise that since supper we have gone to another all-time low? In the last half hour the barometer has descended another six millibars!'

I took the precaution of blocking up the door with some Inca snow masonry, but they were thin blocks and half an hour later, sitting in bed with whisky and a precious wisp of tobacco, I could hear the renewed blizzard tearing and howling outside.

We were taking turns to dip into Apsley Cherry-Garrard's *The Worst Journey in the World* and had adopted his use of the

Julian talking to a light-mantled sooty albatross.

Fur seal pup sunning itself amongst the scrap metal the Argentinians never took from Leith Harbour.

Looking down the Brögger Glacier to Undine South Harbour and Annenkov Island, 25 miles offshore.

The author in the snowcave, after having a look outside.
(*Photo by Julian Freeman-Attwood*)

Brian outside, fighting a classic South Georgia blizzard.

A magical evening near the top of Mt Carse. The Novosilski Glacier is far below; 25 miles to the north-west the great dome of Mt Paget bestrides the island.

Brian nears the top of Mt Carse as the sun sets over the Southern Ocean.

The following morning on the Novosilski Glacier, skiing home from Mt Carse. The route on the mountain took the faint ridge descending towards the camera.

Back at Royal Bay - the view from the hut across Moltke Harbour.

Julian makes way for a mature bull elephant seal in Royal Bay. The seal is reversing indignantly towards the security of the water.

A small gathering of king penguins at Royal Bay.

The main rookery at St Andrew's Bay after a night of heavy rain.

The young gentoo penguins at home above Doris Bay. The next bay round is St Andrew's, with Cape Vakop on the far right.

Cumberland East Bay with Nordenskjöld Peak (left) and Mt Roots rising above the Nordenskjöld Glacier.

A calm evening in Cumberland East Bay, with lenticular clouds bringing promise of the next storm.

verb 'to blizz', establishing our own meteorological 'Blizzing Scale'. On Thursday we had '100 per cent blizzing', which meant that it was impossible to see the rocks thirty yards away on the far side of the scoop. We kept the peephole closed with an ice axe shaft and every time someone removed it to have a look outside, a fine spray of spindrift jetted through the hole into the lobby.

That afternoon there was a triumphant shout from the north wing. At least it was as close to a shout as Kees ever came and the message was clear: after ten days' nurturing in his sleeping bag and many sessions over the gas stove, the Aaton had at last shown a flicker of life. Filming could continue. However, for the moment Kees was only cautiously optimistic, urged restraint, and prescribed a full convalescence for the 16 mm camera before it could be exposed again to the elements. So he made do with the inferior video 8 mm when we set off on a climb the next morning.

It was Brian who woke us up at 4 a.m. Apparently the sky was clear, or at least clear enough to nip over the Ross Pass and bag a fine little virgin peak that we had been eyeing up. I started resentfully to get dressed. Julian chose exactly the same moment to get ready and soon our little tent was in chaos. I mislaid a sock, cursed Julian and made him turn out the whole tent. After ranting for another fifteen minutes I eventually found the sock in my sleeping bag. Later I apologised to Julian, who lectured, 'Well, yes, that's all right, but the trouble with losing your temper is that it's contagious . . . everyone starts getting ratty . . . '

'Speak for yourself,' I thought.

A faint white sun half-pierced the clouds as we left, but it did not last long. I took skis, skidding across hard-packed sastrugi, the wind-flaked snow corrugations so cursed by polar explorers when they reached their extreme form up to three feet high. Julian followed on snow shoes. Brian, Lindsay and Kees came a little later. By the time Julian, Brian and I had regrouped on the far side of the pass, visibility was drastically reduced and we made our way up the chosen snow ridge in a virtual whiteout. Lindsay, for reasons best known to himself, took Kees round the back, leading him up quite a steep ice face and doing a flanking movement on to the summit.

Kees arrived on top in 100 per cent blizzing conditions but still

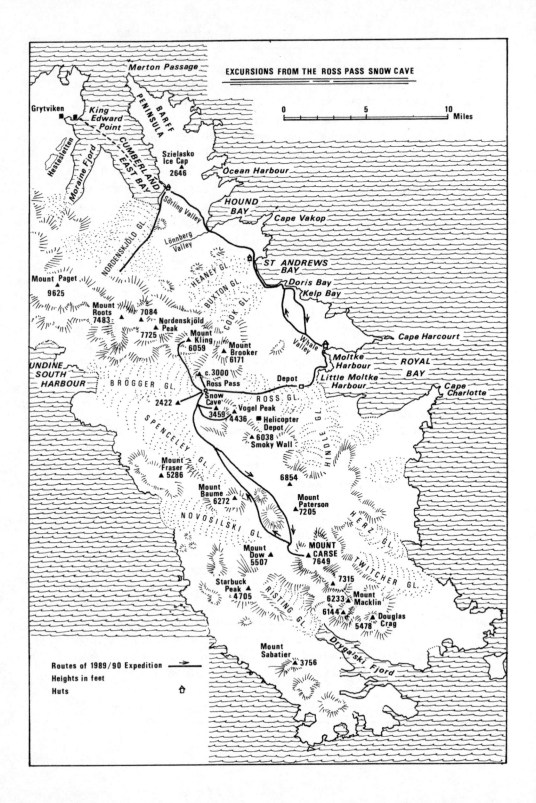

EXCURSIONS FROM THE ROSS PASS SNOW CAVE

0   5   10 Miles

Merton Passage

Grytviken

King Edward Point

BARFF PENINSULA

Hestesletten

Moraine Fjord

CUMBERLAND EAST BAY

Szielasko Ice Cap
2646

Sörling Valley

Ocean Harbour

HOUND BAY

Cape Vakop

Lönnberg Valley

ST ANDREWS BAY

Doris Bay

Kelp Bay

NORDENSKJÖLD GL.

Mount Paget
9625

HEANEY GL.

BUXTON GL.

COOK GL.

Whale Valley

Cape Harcourt

Mount Roots
7483

7084

Nordenskjöld Peak

7725

Mount Kling
6059

Mount Brooker
6171

Moltke Harbour

ROYAL BAY

UNDINE SOUTH HARBOUR

BRÖGGER GL.

c.3000
Ross Pass

Snow Cave

2422

Depot

Little Moltke Harbour

ROSS GL.

Cape Charlotte

Vogel Peak
3459 4436

Helicopter Depot

SPENCELEY GL.

6038
Smoky Wall

HINDLE GL.

Mount Fraser
5286

6854

Mount Baume
6272

Mount Paterson
7205

HERZ GL.

NOVOSILSKI GL.

Mount Dow
5507

MOUNT CARSE
7649

MOUNT TWITCHER

GL.

Starbuck Peak
4705

RISTING GL.

7315

6233

6144

Mount Macklin

Douglas Crag
5478

Drygalski Fjord

Mount Sabatier
3756

Routes of 1989/90 Expedition

Heights in feet

Huts

managed to video us, with the summit flag flapping and tugging like a wild animal. Then we left. Brian and Lindsay escorted Kees while Julian and I went ahead. The descent went quite well until I had to collect my skis. Then all hell was let loose as I slithered and stumbled, completely disorientated, not knowing whether I was going up or down, blasted off balance by the wind. Once we were back on the plateau it was a little easier and Julian directed me from behind, trying to keep me on a compass bearing. My glasses were completely iced up, so I had to take them off and bare my eyes to see. That meant skiing bent, head twisted sideways with windward eye firmly shut and the other squinting at the featureless ground.

I followed Julian's instructions blindly, veering left and right as told. Once he failed to cancel an instruction to steer right, until eventually there was a distant shout from way over to my left. 'Where are hell are you going, Venables? You're heading straight down the Brögger for the sea!' He got me back on target and soon we hit the marker wands at the edge of the scoop. At 11 a.m. we were back in the cave, removing sodden clothes and nursing sore eyeballs, stung raw by the blizzard.

'The Thing' or 'The Blob', as we called our first summit, was hardly a major achievement, but at least we had climbed something, getting everyone to an unequivocal summit and some video footage in the can. The struggle back to the cave had also been quite exhilarating, reminding us just how difficult it could be to move on South Georgia – even a two-mile journey, unladen, on familiar ground, returning to a secure base. Small wonder that the SAS landing on the Fortuna Glacier in 1982 was such a disaster.

At that stage, in April 1982, the British government was hoping still to avoid a full scale war, using the recapture of South Georgia as a warning to Argentina to leave the Falklands. It has been suggested that the SAS, fearing that South Georgia would be their only chance for glorious action, were determined to make the most of this opportunity. The Commander of Land Forces, Guy Sheridan, noted in his diary: 'In my orders to D Sqdn I had advised, in my experience, to avoid glaciers like the plague. I believe with the prevailing weather at this time of year and appallingly treacherous going on crevassed glaciers, this is a bad choice.'

Sheridan was an extremely experienced mountaineer, best known for a recent gruelling ski tour through remote Himalayan country in the depths of winter. But the D Sqdn mountain troop was determined to go its own heroic way, insisting that a more direct approach to Stromness Bay would risk detection by the Argentinians. So sixteen men were plucked suddenly from the shelter of a warship and 'inserted' on a strange, remote glacier as another winter blizzard moved in from the west. They were weighed down by full survival gear, guns and ammunition and they faced a journey of over ten miles. In perfect weather their plan might well have succeeded, but in normal South Georgian conditions it was virtually doomed to failure. They were battered mercilessly by winds gusting to 100 knots, they fell repeatedly into crevasses, their tents were ripped to shreds and two helicopters crashed trying to rescue them the next day. Miraculously no one was even seriously injured and in a brilliant piece of bold flying, heavily overloaded, the third helicopter managed to evacuate all sixteen men back to the safety of HMS *Antrim*.

Kees finally had his chance to do some 16 mm filming on January 15th. For three days since climbing The Thing we had been settled back into the snowcave routine, but at eight o'clock that morning Julian announced that the weather had cleared. Apathy gave way to delight and breakfast was delayed while we rushed, slithering, up on to the plateau, dragging out socks, jackets, sleeping bags and mattresses to dry in the precious sunshine. Then we posed for Kees, putting on harnesses, coiling ropes, uncoiling ropes, putting on sun cream and goggles, stepping into ski bindings or snow-shoes, setting off across the glacier, coming back across the glacier two minutes later, filming everything ten times, from ten different angles, with an endless variety of cutaway details for Kees to play with when he eventually started editing in London.

Brian and Lindsay later volunteered magnanimously to stage a dramatic climb up a tiny cliff just across the windscoop from our front door, giving Kees a wealth of technical detail to be fudged into the final film. Meanwhile Julian and I went skiing. For the first time we headed south to the line of nunataks – the spiky rock islands where Duncan Carse had advised us to camp. We crossed over a little pass, descended on to the Spenceley Glacier and traversed round a corner to have a look at Vogel Peak, the mountain which we had approached from the wrong side two weeks earlier. Here, as I had suspected, was the best route up the mountain – a glaciated flank which would be quite feasible if the weather held one more day.

We returned to the cave and after lunch I did some more skiing on the hill immediately above the windscoop. It gave a glorious descent, culminating in a steep swoop right down on to the frozen lake. On the final session, I climbed a little higher up the hill, zigzagging on skins several hundred feet above the glacier, then stopped to enjoy half an hour's peaceful solitude.

The sky was half-clouded, softening the sunlight and dappling the velvet surface of the Brögger Glacier flowing below me. Beyond the glacier, looking very close but actually twenty-five miles out to sea, lay Annenkov Island, the landmark that had guided Shackleton's navigator, the sea captain Frank Worsley, when he made his landfall in 1916. Today the sea was sleek silver and it was hard to realise that out there the *James Caird* had beat back and forth desperately for two days, battered by Force Eleven winds and giant rollers as the six men, tortured by thirst, rubbed raw by wet salty clothes, bleary with exhaustion, baled for their lives. Unlike the north-east coast, South Georgia's south-western seaboard has few anchorages and in 1916 was virtually uncharted. Most of the coast is icebound and Shackleton was still hoping to creep right round the western tip of South Georgia and sail all the way to the whaling stations.

In the end, desperate to escape the sea, the men dragged their boat ashore at King Haakon Bay just as the pin securing the rudder finally gave way. Shackleton and Worsley decided that the battered craft would never make it right round the coast so they rested three days, gorging themselves on succulent stewed albatross chicks to regain some strength, then set off with the second officer, Tom Crean, on their historic mountain crossing to Stromness, leaving the other three to wait with the shattered boat.

Shackleton was a sailor, not a mountaineer, and his description of the crossing tends to exaggerate heights and distances. For instance, the neck of land now called Shackleton Gap, which he estimated at eight to nine miles is in fact less than four miles wide and only rises a few hundred feet above sea level; the great bergschrund which blocked his route at one point was not a real bergschrund produced by glacial stress, but a typical South Georgian windscoop. One could cite other inaccuracies, but they are irrelevant beside the magnitude of his achievement. No one had ever penetrated the interior of the island and no map existed. Shackleton, Crean and Worsley had to rely on a sketchy coastal chart, supplemented by hazy memory and intuition. They realised, when they looked down the far side of Shackleton Gap, that the inlet beyond was Possession Bay, not Stromness. This was to be no simple crossing from coast to coast, but a gruelling eastward traverse over what are now called the Murray Snowfield, the Crean Glacier, the Fortuna Glacier and the König Glacier, until at last only a short stretch of snow-covered hills separated them from Stromness Bay.

Shackleton knew that if he failed to reach help, his three companions waiting at King Haakon Bay would probably die, along with the twenty-two men marooned 850 miles away on Elephant Island. He only agreed to stop for the briefest meal pauses and never once slept during those thirty-six hours. He must have been experiencing more intensely than ever before that almost euphoric sensation of total concentration, sublime simplicity and heightened awareness that sustains men at the limit of survival. It is hardly surprising that he wrote afterwards:

> I have no doubt that Providence guided us, not only across the snowfields, but also across the storm-white seas that separated Elephant Island from our landing-place on South Georgia. I know that during that long and racking march of thirty-six hours over the unnamed mountains and glaciers of South Georgia it seemed to me that we were four, not three.

He goes on to confess '"the dearth of human words, the roughness of mortal speech" in trying to describe things intangible'; but the experience inspired his contemporary, T. S. Eliot, to write the evocative passage in 'The Waste Land' – 'Who is the third who walks always beside you?' – amplifying the religious overtones hinted at in Shackleton's own account. He and his companions do seem to have experienced a powerful feeling that some higher force had decreed the extraordinary, improbable sequence of events that led to the crossing of South Georgia. Perhaps 'Providence' also intended that Shackleton should die here six years later, ensuring that his name would be for ever linked with the island.

Shackleton may be the name that springs to mind, but others have made their mark on the island. In recent years the name most closely associated with South Georgia has been that of Duncan Carse.

Carse decided as a young man that he wanted to write, but that first he needed to broaden his experience by travelling. But the only place he wanted to see was Antarctica, 'because there aren't any people there'. With no money, he had to make his way there in devious stages, first working as a seaman on the four-masted barque *Archibald Russell* in the 1932–3 grain race, then, with that valuable apprenticeship behind him, getting a job with the Antarctic research vessel, RRS *Discovery II*. In 1934 he managed to sign off the *Discovery* at Port Stanley and work his way on to the British Grahamland Expedition, spending the next two and a half years exploring the Antarctic Peninsula.

After the War, determined to prove that there was still room in the world for the freelance polar explorer, Carse started to search for an area in need of mapping that was accessible and affordable on a small budget. South Georgia fitted the bill perfectly. With the generous support of Christian Salvesen's whaling ships the island was cheaply accessible from Britain; there was also ready boat transport with the sealers around the coast to the various bays and inlets. Yet, in spite of its industrial infrastructure, the island was still mostly unmapped. The coastal chart was incomplete and the mountains were virtually unknown. When Carse and his four companions arrived for the first survey expedition in 1951, only two previous parties were known to have penetrated the interior: Shackleton's in 1916 and the Kohl-Larsen expedition in 1928–9. Whole glacier systems and mountain ranges lay untouched, still, in 1951, safe from the space satellite's camera, waiting for the traditional explorer to unravel their mysteries.

Carse did for South Georgia what the celebrated mountaineers Tilman and Shipton had done for large areas of the Himalaya. The South Georgia Survey Expeditions were privately organised, paid for by minimal sponsorship, Falklands government funds and whatever goods and services Carse could scrounge from companies. His teams were not paid and had to do the job for the love of it. Apart from boat transport to starting points on the coast, travel was entirely on foot, usually towing sledges. The teams were small; luxuries were few; food and gear were kept to the basic minimum.

Already in the first season, Carse's surveyors began to correct major inaccuracies in the existing 1930s' chart. On the south-west coast major indentations were missing and on the other coast the area around St Andrew's Bay was inaccurate; but the wildest errors were in the central mountains and glaciers. The Ross Pass was aligned at completely the wrong angle, with the Brögger Glacier apparently flowing south-west, instead of due west to Undine South Harbour, which had previously been charted ten miles north of its true position.

Now, looking down the Brögger Glacier, it was hard to believe that less than forty years ago, Carse and his team were the first people ever to tread here and to cross the nunatak ridge to the Spenceley Glacier, subsequently named after the photographer on his third expedition. Carse returned twice with sledging teams to continue working over the island's glaciers, then alone in the 1956–7 season to tidy up the remaining coastal detail before handing over the completed results to the Ordnance Survey.

Talking later to Carse and to some of his companions on those long sledging journeys, I got the impression that he endured company only out of necessity and that, once the main sledging survey was complete, he was perhaps happiest on the fourth expedition, spending weeks alone, yomping around the coast, or at sea with his sealing friends in the *Albatros*, *Diaz* and *Petrel* – the boats which now lie, half-wrecked, at Grytviken. The island, which he knew and loved better than anyone, seems to have become increasingly a source of solace; and even though the survey was complete, he returned in 1961, hoping to stay eighteen months, completely alone.

On February 22nd, 1961, Carse was landed from HMS *Owen* at a sheltered cove, next to Ducloz Head, on the south-west coast. Here, on the one and a half square miles of scree, rock, tussock and glacier that Carse had leased for one shilling, he set up his hut and prepared to spend the next eighteen months in complete solitude. He had arranged for sealing vessels to deliver mail occasionally, but placed his red post box out of sight so that he would never actually have to meet the postman.

By the end of March the hut was complete and Carse was able to move out of his tent. But on April 5th he fell and ripped the ligaments in his left leg. For a month he was laid up and he was only just starting to recover when the tidal wave struck at dawn on May 20th. Carse was asleep in his hut and woke to find himself in the open, barefoot, surrounded by wreckage, swirled around as the cove 'emptied and filled like a washbasin'. Tussock grass had been ripped from the cliffs forty feet up from the beach. The hut was gone but miraculously Carse managed to find his tents, sleeping bags, stoves, fuel, matches and food rations. Later he salvaged skis, ski sticks, scraps of building material and some of his tools; his twelve-foot dinghy was also intact.

It was now winter and no sealing vessel would call for at least four months. His dinghy couldn't compare with Shackleton's *James Caird* for seaworthiness and, from this remote camp, hemmed in by the main wall of the Allardyce Range, it would have been virtually impossible for a fit man to travel overland to the whaling stations. For a man dragging a crippled leg, it was out of the question. So Carse had to dig in to face the long dark nights of winter alone, deprived of most of his possessions, holed up in a cold tent.

The only written account of those winter months is Carse's unpublished radio script, which portrays with alarming frankness the stress of lonely survival:

> I was a very frightened man – a very unhappy man: something had happened for which there was no accounting, and I needed an explanation. But there wasn't one – not one that made sense. I had simply to go on living, and for no very good reason, because that was all that was left me.

Like others in similar situations, he insisted on discipline:

> I committed myself to a minimum acceptable standard of living,
> no squalor – regular food and so on – and I swore that I'd never
> relax that discipline. I had to do this, because I'm very vulner-
> able to discomfort.

But, in spite of the discipline, he was plagued by anxiety during
those long winter nights, terrified that there might be a repeat of
that irrational freak wave. He tried to improve his quarters, using
his dinghy to make a lean-to hut, rather like Frank Wild and the
other survivors of the *Endurance* on Elephant Island. By July 6th it
was complete, secure and sealed with blankets, packing cases,
roofing felt scraps and tussock grass; but when he moved in he
found the silence oppressive: 'I'd sound-proofed the Lodge, and I
could hear nothing at all – not even the surf on the Outer Rocks.'
So he moved back into the tent.

Spring finally came and at last, on September 13th, 116 days
after the Wave, he spotted the sealer, *Albatros*, steaming down the
coast past Ducloz Head. But she was steaming away south.

> So I waved: I was on the skyline – I was wearing a red sweater,
> they were bound to see me. But they didn't, and I began to shout
> – which was pretty half-witted, when you come to think of it. I
> went on shouting for some minutes: and the *Albatros* went on
> steaming – and nobody was paying any attention – and I went
> berserk. I simply tore up and down my skyline, stumbling and
> tripping, breaking through the crust to my thighs – falling over
> and getting up again – arms and legs like a windmill: and I was
> screaming obscenities – blasphemies – gibberish. If they don't
> see me, they'll hear me: I'll make them! But they didn't; and the
> *Albatros* went on steaming, into the lobe of the pack – and
> through it – and out the other side, and out of range. So I gave
> up; and made my way back to Last Camp – and I flopped.

He boiled himself a mug of powdered milk, his 'cure-all for
emotional crisis' and sat down to smoke a pipe. Later that day he
heard the putter-putter of a small motorboat putting into the cove,

rushed up to Lookout Bluff and saw another sealer, the *Petrel*, waiting offshore. A few minutes later he left with his rescuers, and like so many people trying to recall moments of emotional catharsis he has

> ... no recollection at all of what we said. But I remember getting into the pram – and being rowed across the cove – and the boatman's offering me a cigarette – and the sun coming out, and the whole world suddenly golden-warm and glad and – and almost singing. And I'd never seen the Cove looking so beautiful, and I loved it and couldn't bear to leave it, and I wanted to cry: and I knew I'd have to come back and do it all over again – without the Wave.

Sitting on my perch above the Ross Pass, I could see where it had all happened, where the mountains tumbled into the shimmering surface of Undine South Harbour. Ducloz Head was the furthest point, fifteen miles away. Just inside the point, protected apparently by an encircling arm of dark rocks, over which the Wave had smashed, there was a tiny patch of silver – the Cove where Carse had spent those seven months. It did look sublimely beautiful and very, very lonely.

That evening the view down to Undine South Harbour remained clear, and for the first time in days we enjoyed a sunset. The prevailing wind had swung to the east, and only a hint of cloud drifted idly on the far side of the Ross Pass. Anxious to make the most of the opportunity, we went early to bed and at midnight Brian was up making the tea. The rest of us surfaced at 1.00 a.m. and by 2.30 a.m. on January 16th we were on our way to attempt Vogel Peak.

Now that Julian and I had reconnoitred the approach we made no mistakes, travelling quickly round to our route on the southwest flank. Julian, still not completely reconciled to the hostile mountains, reminded us that he would turn back if 'the weather manked in' – but the weather was kind.

We started in the dark, with only the faint gleam of a half-moon supplementing our torch bulbs. Brian, Julian and I took skis, while Lindsay and Kees followed on snowshoes. From the pass on the nunatak ridge we had a beautiful swoop on hard frozen snow down to the Spenceley Glacier, then a steady climb on skins up into the glacier bay at the foot of Vogel. Cloud was banked up on the far side of the Salvesen Range, but evaporated harmlessly as it poured over to our side. As the dawn glow brightened from purple to pink, everyone warmed to the day's work.

Kees agreed graciously to stay at the foot of the mountain, filming with a long lens while 'the mountaineers' rushed ahead, starting the climb at 5.00 a.m. Brian, who was normally violently opposed to the distractions of filming, volunteered cheerfully to carry the lightweight video camera for additional filming on the route. Julian was now committed to the summit and was enthralled by our surroundings. For a year now he had been studying the map and knew the spot height of every unnamed peak on the island. 'Look there's 6854 – isn't she wonderful? And look – those two, on the far side of the Spenceley, must be 5018 and 5680. Sound country!' But highest praise was reserved for an elegant peak named after some explorer, Fraser, which also happened to be Elaine's surname.

Our route up Vogel Peak wound its way between ice cliffs and crevasses. The technical difficulties were not extreme but we travelled through exciting scenery. Halfway up the mountain we had to traverse along the lower lip of a huge crevasse fringed above by giant stalactites, spiked with hoar frost, reminding me of similar formations in the equally damp climate of Africa's Mountains of the Moon. A snow bridge and a steep little ice wall got us over the crevasse and above that we found another steep wall of ice leading to more crevasses, a broad snow ridge and, finally, a very steep wall of hoar frost. We took it in turns to squeeze up a chimney ramp through the wall and, a few minutes later, at 7.30 in the morning, we were all on the summit, holding up the expedition flag with Julian's logo painted silver on green silk: *Southern Ocean Mountaineering Expedition supports Antarctica as a World Park.*

Already the wind was veering back to the west and the sky was clouding over, casting a dull yellow light over the mountains. In the best South Georgia tradition we had snatched our mountain during a brief clearing, reaching the second summit ever to be climbed on the main divide of the Salvesen Range. The first, Mt Paterson, was climbed by Carse's team in 1956.

We celebrated back at the snowcave with Marks & Spencer's fruit cake and a hot punch of rosehip tea, lemon, honey and whisky. We were pleased with our ascent, but on the way back over the nunatak pass it had been impossible not to glance south, up that long wide corridor of the Spenceley Glacier. The mountains at the far end of the Salvesen Range had looked strangely close in the flat grey light and for the first time we had seen the white dome of Mt Carse, waiting twelve miles away.

10

At the Eleventh Hour

Mt Carse was one of the most impractical objectives we could have chosen, stuck right down at the southern end of the island, further than almost any other peak from King Edward Point. But mountaineering is by its nature illogical, and the mountain's very inaccessibility made it attractive. The fact that it was the highest unclimbed peak on the island made it doubly attractive. In retrospect we would have done best to take heavy, robust pyramid tents and sledges, enabling us to move steadily up the glaciers instead of holing up at the static base on the Ross Pass. But, given the uncertainty about sea and helicopter transport, and the knowledge that all equipment had to be carried eventually back to Cumberland East Bay, we had opted for a compromise, taking just lightweight tents and no sledges; hence the ice palace.

By the time we eventually climbed Vogel Peak, we had been sixteen days at the Ross Pass and we only had a week's food left. So far we had not ventured more than three or four miles from the snowcave and it was now far too late to lay a depot or camp closer to Mt Carse. As the barometer plummeted and we settled underground again, hopes of reaching the mountain faded. It now looked as though we would be lucky to achieve anything more before returning to Cumberland East Bay. If we did get another break, Julian was all for trying Mt Kling – a fine unclimbed peak much closer, just north of The Thing – but even that was now looking doubtful.

Julian occupied the moral high ground each evening in the south wing. After supper with the others in the damp north wing, we would return to our tent, build up a good fug with a gas stove, then enjoy the day's cigarette. The tobacco was Julian's, because he had been careful to conserve stocks while I used up all my ration at Royal Bay. So each evening I had to grovel abjectly for a drag on his matchstick-thin roll-up and endure jibes at my profligacy. There were also friendly jibes at my dogged optimism. Julian had virtually reconciled himself to achieving no more climbs in the southern part of the island, settling for our limited achievement on Vogel. His patience was running out and he scorned my hopes for a last-minute dash to Carse: 'Well, if you want to be stuck ten miles up the Spenceley Glacier in a snowhole for five days with no food . . . trapped by a westerly blizz . . . lost in a whiteout . . . fine! But I suppose you Everest heroes need to keep achieving.' He was only joking, but I suppose there was a grain of truth in it.

Lindsay possessed inexhaustible patience and had gone into semi-hibernation with his bumper crossword book. On Himalayan expeditions he is always the last to leave base camp, often waiting until the winter snows drive him down to the valley in a desperate Retreat from Moscow. He would hang on as long as possible; but Kees and Brian were now talking about cutting our losses and heading back to Cumberland East Bay, to see what we could achieve there.

Three days passed. It rained and the snowcave dripped incessantly, saving us the trouble of sliding down to the lake to fetch water. Then it grew colder and we blocked the door again as the blizzing scale stuck at 100 per cent. The food dwindled and I began to look forward to our escape to the coast. Then, on Saturday January 20th, the weather cleared slightly. We were back to the hoping, gambling, dithering, evaluating game. Tempers ran high. Brian cursed Kees for keeping us hanging around filming when we could have done a small climb. Julian and I burnt the rubbish, hunched over the flames like tramps. Kees suddenly insisted, 'If you want to get your environmental angle, then this is a good thing to film.'

'What – burning some rubbish?' Julian snapped.

'Yes – that we show this problem,' lilted back the Dutchman.

Our ecology spokesman went berserk: 'Whenever I suggest anything environmental, Kees just squashes it, saying that it's irrelevant or not part of the story. But now that *he* suddenly wants to make an environmental point, it's all different. I'm not going to make any more suggestions.'

It snowed at midday but another slight clearing in the afternoon allowed us to go out and conquer Point 2422 – the last untouched pinnacle on the nunatak ridge. It gave us some exercise and Kees some action footage. Brian, Julian and I reached the summit at dusk, while Lindsay ploughed his lonely furrow to a twin peak three feet lower.

The wind was now starting to veer round to the east, and the barometer was rising with the hint of a genuine fine spell. At the last moment, after all the procrastination of recent days, we seemed to be getting one final chance. We still had enough food to stretch for two days, and if it was fine in the morning we could attempt one more climb. At supper Brian and I discussed the possibility of dashing over to Mt Carse. It would be a long risky journey, with no reserves if we got cut off by another blizzard, but if we took the little tent we would have adequate shelter. The best way to avoid getting trapped was to travel fast, with skis. That ruled out Lindsay and Kees; and Julian had already made his opinion about Mt Carse quite clear.

The alarm woke me from a deep sleep at 4 a.m. the next morning. I left the tent, put on boots, went to open the front door and climbed the steps to the plateau. There was a cold wind from the east, but most of the summits were clear and out to the south-west there was not a cloud in the sky. I went back inside to wake up the others and Brian asked, 'So, are we going for our big ski tour up the Spenceley Glacier?'

We ate our breakfast quickly and packed to leave. I felt a bit uneasy over our unilateral decision and Lindsay seemed disgruntled at being left to attempt a nearer goal. Kees, anxious to know what he could film, asked, 'Are you going to climb Kling, Lindsay?'

'What? I don't know; I've only just woken up.' Julian was similarly rebuffed with the old Griffin formula, 'Let's play it by ear.'

'But I don't want to "play it by ear",' he groaned. 'I want to make a plan.'

It was a relief to escape at 7.00 a.m. The sun was up, the snow was sparkling and the two of us were setting off on an exciting journey. In half an hour we climbed across to the nunatak pass, where we stopped to remove skins for the descent on to the Spenceley Glacier. Our white road stretched far ahead, up to a high pass, with Mt Carse just visible beyond, twelve miles from where we stood.

Once again we swooped down on to the bay below Vogel; but this time, instead of turning left, we kept straight ahead, skirting round another nunatak ridge, then putting on skins for the long climb up the main highway of the Spenceley Glacier. Now that we were moving uphill Brian pulled ahead, setting a fast pace as we climbed for the next three hours. Weather and conditions were perfect. On our left the cloud poured harmlessly over the poetically-named Smoky Wall, but the sky overhead was clear blue. I had never skied in such immaculate isolation and, catching up with Brian at a rest stop, I shouted proudly, 'They can keep Verbier and Val-d'Isère – all that pushing and shoving on ski lifts, like Monday morning on the Underground.'

The freedom was exhilarating, but also slightly frightening for we were travelling further and further from help. On New Year's Day, 1952 the geologist, Alec Trendall, had fallen unroped into a crevasse quite near here, dislocating a knee. Carse and the other men managed to haul him out but it took four days to drag him on a sledge all the way back to Cumberland East Bay. The accident cut short their exploration of the Spenceley Glacier and it was only on his third expedition that Carse completed the sledging route through from the Ross Pass to Drygalski Fjord at the southern tip of the island.

On 28th January, 1956 the eight-man team left Royal Bay. They spent several days ferrying loads over the Ross Pass in abysmal conditions but on February 8th the weather improved as they got established on the Spenceley Glacier. Four days later, in perfect weather, they crossed the pass at the head of the glacier, mapping the new territory as they went. Keith Warburton, the doctor, Stan Paterson, one of the surveyors, with Tom Price and John Cunningham, both well-known mountaineers, made a detour to climb the highest peak so far ascended on the island – the 7205-ft Mt

Paterson. Then the whole team descended to the Novosilski Glacier and pushed south, linking further glaciers that gave a passage right through to Drygalski Fjord.

They were only a few miles from the planned rendezvous with a sealing vessel when a blizzard struck on February 22nd, pinning them down for seven days in their tents, fearful that the fabric, scoured thin after three months in the field, would rip to shreds.

Now Brian and I were retracing their steps, all too aware that we too could find ourselves trapped by a break in the weather. The difference was that we had only enough fuel to melt snow for three or four days, and food for just two. So there was a certain urgency as we pressed on towards the head of the glacier, framed on the left by Mt Paterson and on the right by Mt Baume, named after another member of the 1955–6 expedition. At eleven o'clock we reached the pass and there, framed in the vee of a further pass, was our mountain.

We took off our skins and Brian shot some video as I started down the far side of the pass. I weaved a line through ice towers down into the upper basin of the Novosilski Glacier. Then it was on with skins for the climb to the final pass. It was midday now and the sky was a dark blue and the glacier was hot white against the green and purple sea. Only three other parties had ever been here before: Carse in 1956, a BAS geological survey in 1974 and the Joint Services Expedition in 1982. The 1982 team had also been pinned down by blizzards and had been driven back from attempting Mt Carse.

At one o'clock we reached the final pass and studied the mountain. Our only previous knowledge had been from distant photos and it was now clear that the left-hand ridge – the East Ridge – was not as easy as we had thought. We would do better to attempt the North-West Ridge on the right, and it looked as though we could start the ridge by taking glacier slopes round on the west side. In the meantime we could pitch the tent under a rock buttress on the near side of the ridge.

We had to descend about 800 feet to the campsite. The initial slope was quite steep and I skied very deliberately, knees well bent, carving huge sweeping turns, determined not to be toppled by my heavy rucksack. Then the slope eased off into a glorious wind-whistling Schuss, skimming the last mile in a few minutes. At 1.30 we arrived at a small hollow below the rock buttress. By 2.30 the little tent was pitched, guy lines secured by skis and ski-poles, valance safely weighed down with huge blocks of snow. Inside our warm nest we relaxed with boots off and prepared some lunch.

'Six and a half hours from the snowcave – quite quick, weren't we? Now we've got time to have a good sleep and leave really early for the climb. How about midnight?' I suggested.

'I think we should go now.'

'What?'

'Well, after we've had some rest,' Brian qualified his urgency. 'But the longer we stay here, the more chance there is of getting caught by the weather.'

'I suppose so,' I agreed reluctantly. We had come thirteen miles and crossed three passes; reversing that route straight in the face of a westerly blizzard could be impossible.

Brian elaborated on his plan. We would leave at five in the afternoon as temperatures began to drop again, re-freezing the snow. If things went well we ought to complete the 4000-foot climb before darkness fell at 9.30. We could descend by head-torch, have a rest back at the tent, then set off home, getting back to the snowcave some time the next morning, before the weather had a chance to break.

It was all very different from the Shisha Pangma expedition two years earlier, when Brian had seemed so negative and obstructive. Now he was the one with the initiative, the tactician, taking the mountain by storm before it knew what had happened. And of course he was right. After weeks of festering inactivity we had to grab the moment. There would be time to sleep later.

That same afternoon, Lindsay, Julian and Kees were busy sixteen miles away in the Allardyce Range. When Brian and I had left at seven in the morning the scene had been tense. Julian was looking forward to the attempt on an unclimbed peak with a man who has become something of a legend in mountaineering circles. But, as I remembered from my own outings with Lindsay, there was not much chance of hurrying. Firstly, as Julian recalls, 'Lindsay's crampons had to be done up. Straps, yards long, wound round and round until the foot was trussed up better than any chicken. Then, finally, Lindsay emerged from the snowcave and declared his intention to begin.'

They roped up, with Kees in tow, and headed north past the Ross Pass, skirting some huge crevasses below The Thing, then climbing up into the broad bay at the head of the Brögger Glacier, below Mt Kling. 'Here we found a suitable spot to leave Kees and his cameras, but it turned out that the poor chap was left in a maze of hidden crevasses.' Lindsay told him not to move until they returned. Then the two climbers continued up the glacier, leaving two strategic marker wands and noting compass bearings in case they returned in a whiteout.

By late morning they had climbed up on to the South-West Ridge of Mt Kling, where they looked across at the immense South Face of Nordenskjöld Peak, a diversion which prompted 'endless Griffin talk about possible routes, with few conclusions except the usual "just play it by ear, old fruit". Playing it by ear seemed to include about a month's ridge work to the summit, by which time one would have been blown into the sea. But there was another fine sight. Just below us, between Nordenskjöld, and Kling, there is a wide saddle. The cloud was banked up on the east just level with the saddle and spilling over our side. Our "cloud fall" poured continuously down on to the Brögger Glacier, two thousand feet below, where it dissipated like spray.'

They returned to work, climbing along the ridge and on to a 500-ft face of steep, brittle ice. They had only two ice screws between them, so just one anchor on each belay. They alternated leads for four long pitches, steepening to 65 degrees and leading to the base of the summit 'castle'. It was Julian's turn to lead the final seventy-foot wall. There was a choice of thin crumbling ice or rotten rock. He chose the rock, first placing his only ice screw as token protection in the last solid ice just below the wall. 'I remember thinking how Brian would have liked that pitch – no protection and the mountain threatening to disintegrate around you.'

So the man who had been plagued by doubts at Christmas ended up doing a bold lead up the only piece of serious technical climbing on the entire expedition. At the top Julian found himself on a knife-edge summit with a truly vertical precipice dropping to the north. 'But it wasn't quite the summit, because just above was the most incredible tottering ice tower I had ever seen. I brought up Lindsay, who paused at the top, looked up at the tower and said, "Well, fuck a black pig." I'm not sure what pigs had to do with it, but we did give the tower a go. Each stroke of the axe resulted in a large hole and hundreds of bits of ice cascading down into the cloudfall. Convincing ourselves that said tower was in imminent danger of breaking off completely, we settled for the highest solid bit of mountain, unfurled our Antarctica World Park flag and sat down to take in the view.'

Only the most ardent pedant could dispute that Julian and Lindsay reached the 6059-ft summit of Mt Kling. Later I saw Lindsay's photograph of Julian, flag and view south right down the Salvesen Range to the distant white dome of Mt Carse. At that moment Brian and I were just setting out on our climb.

At five o'clock we zipped up the tent and left. Now that we were on foot, not skis, there was more chance of breaking through into concealed crevasses, so we roped up for the start of our climb. It took fifteen minutes to descend the glacier to the toe of the North-West Ridge, then we were climbing – up an ice ramp, weaving between crevasses, side-stepping green chasms, following white troughs hidden in the folds of the mountain, stabbing with crampons up a long slope of blackened ice, ploughing a gentler rise of soft snow . . . but the technical details were not important; what counted on this climb was just to be there, alone at the southern tip of South Georgia on an evening of rare tranquillity.

The clear southern light still surprised me, contracting distance so that one could hardly believe that the Novosilski Glacier stretched fully ten miles, dropping 3500 feet, before it melted into the sea. Ice merged imperceptibly with ocean and beyond the coast floating icebergs were hardly distinguishable from the tiny Nordic Jonassen Rocks and Nilsen Island, or the Anglo-Saxon Pickersgill Islands, fifteen miles out to sea.

Immediately below us dagger shadows of surrounding peaks elongated across the velvet glacier, then disappeared as mist closed in. But it was a friendly mist, giving a romantic soft focus to the pink sunlight. I, for once, was in the lead, kicking steps triumphantly up a steep snow face, heading for what appeared to be a slight saddle behind a rock tower on the ridge. I reckoned that we were at least halfway up the climb, and that from the saddle we should head right along the crest of the ridge.

When I reached the saddle the mist thickened and darkened, causing a moment's confusion as I probed left and right, searching through strange ice towers. Once again, as on Vogel, I was reminded of the Mountains of the Moon, condensing and freezing the mists of the Congo Jungle. Here it was the Southern Ocean but the effect was the same, and it seemed that all the mountain ridges on South Georgia above three or four thousand feet were encrusted with the same fantastic hoar frost sculptures.

Quite soon the mist thinned and we emerged again into the sunlight to find ourselves on a huge snowfield stretching up to more ice towers. Over on our left the identical white icing of Mt Paterson appeared out of the cloud, but far beyond it the Himalayan bulk of Mt Paget dominated the whole island. On the right sharper peaks, all lower than us, crowded down to the sea, now a sheet of gold – radiant, calm and benign, seeming incapable of smashing little boats or battering lone explorers with freak waves.

The sun set but still we were winding our way amongst the towers, hoping, as with all mountains, that the next tower would be the last. The snow had faded to a dull blue-grey, but I could still make out the texture underfoot – little ice flowers, each about two inches across, carpeting the slope in millions. Beyond and below the slope to the east there was still the same cloud sea, tempting one to step off into its soft lapping waves.

The summit of Mt Paterson was now below us and I knew that Carse was only 450 feet higher. Just a few more ice blobs to climb round and we would be there. Luckily Brian was flagging a little, at the end of a 4000-ft climb preceded by six and a half hours' skiing, so I could just keep him in sight and take the odd photo. Then at last I saw the South-East Ridge closing in from the right to meet our flower towers. Brian was waiting just below the top, videoing me as I came up to join him, hoping that the camera would register something in the twilight. 'Well done. Up you go, then, and I'll get you on this last bit.'

So, while he filmed, I continued up the last corridor, which took me between walls of ice flowers straight on to the summit.

Two minutes later Brian appeared on top and I photographed him, a little red figure in the last glimmer of daylight, with the whole island stretched out beyond him to the north-west, a long chain of mountains curving round past Shackleton's coast – Undine South Harbour, Jossac Bight, King Haakon Bay – and on to the far north-west peninsula first discovered 215 years earlier by Captain Cook. Brian joined me and, like Julian's wry hero, Tilman, we 'forgot ourselves so much as to shake hand on it'. I took some more pictures of him with ice axe raised against the orange glow to the west, far out in an infinite expanse of ocean. 'See out there,' he pointed 'about a hundred miles out to the west there's a bank of cloud on the sea. That's the next blizz waiting to move in.'

Even in this still, fine weather there was a cutting wind on top, so we hurried back down into the shelter of the corridor, just below the summit, to have a rest and something to eat. I was shivering and chewing determinedly at the last frozen chocolate when Brian announced triumphantly, 'I brought us a little treat.'

'The marzipan! I was looking for that the other day – searching the larder shelves.'

'Ah, well – you have to prepare for these little outings, and I had to make sure the others wouldn't get their hands on it.'

We ate the entire half-pound block at one sitting, pumping back some calories to try and revive aching muscles starved of blood sugar. Then we left, rushing down by the last remnants of daylight, peering through the gloom for faint marks of our ascent, running in a bent-knee crouch, legs well apart to stop crampon points catching on a trouser leg and sending one somersaulting out of control.

We had reached the summit at 9.30 p.m. We started the descent at about 9.45 p.m. and stopped only once, halfway down, to put on head torches. By about 11.30 we were back in the tent, blissfully horizontal, deliciously warm in our down sleeping bags and relishing the rare sensation of pure physical tiredness. Brian decreed generously that we could have a few hours' sleep and delay the return journey till dawn. He stayed awake long enough for a mug of tea but by the time the soup was ready he was fast asleep. I managed a few sips, then I too sank heavily to sleep.

The slave driver kicked me awake at four o'clock the next morning. There was now a vicious wind pummelling the tent and I had no desire to go outside, so I dozed for another forty-five minutes until Brian forced me to make the breakfast tea. Then, one at a time in the cramped space, we prepared to leave. I crawled first out of the tent, relieved to see that the reality outside was not half as bad as it had sounded. True, there was a violent wind which had forced spindrift through the flysheet zip at Brian's end of the tent, filling the porch with densely packed powder, but it was a local funnelled wind still blowing from the east. Over the sea to the west the sky was blue.

I dug out Brian's snow-packed porch, rescuing his rucksack and boots, then started to dismantle the tent, glad that he was still inside to stop the wild thing taking off. After a numb fumble to pack rucksacks and put on skis, we were away by seven o'clock.

For the return journey we took a slightly simpler route, with just one pass to cross to get back on to the main drag of the Spenceley Glacier. First we had to reach the central junction of the Novosilski Glacier and to get there we had to descend a thousand feet. What a fantastic start to the day, racing seawards, with the wind behind, powering our skimming flight over the glacier! All too soon it was over and we started the long climb north, back up to the head of the Spenceley Glacier. But that is the essence of ski-touring and the long climbs are rewarded with more glorious descent. On this sort of glacier terrain skis are by far the best way of getting around, yet this simple truth was ignored perversely by both Shackleton and Scott during their laboured attempts to reach the South Pole. Shackleton's bold 1909 attempt came within a hair's breadth of disaster; Scott pushed on further in 1912, reaching the Pole with reserves dangerously low and then, on the return, had appalling luck with the weather. With skis the tragedy might have been averted.

Of course our outing to Mt Carse was not remotely comparable to the great epic journeys to the Pole. Nevertheless, it had been quite committing and we were glad to have the speed of skis, particularly on the exhilarating trundle back down the Spenceley Glacier, covering in forty-five minutes the long road which had taken nearly three hours to climb the previous morning.

It was the final crossing below Vogel Peak and back over the nunatak ridge that gave us the concluding drama – the malignant blasts hurling us to the ground, snapping open ski bindings, forcing us to struggle with crampons, flinging me flat on my face, stinging my eyeballs with ice darts, reducing me to the ultimate ignominy of crawling on my hands and knees. All Brian's Scottish and Antarctic mountain experience seemed to come to the fore as he dragged me over the pass and got us safely back on the right track. It was a sobering end to our journey, but it also seemed appropriate that the last mile of our thirty-mile round trip to Mt Carse and back should be done in time-honoured South Georgian tradition – following a compass bearing blindly through a white-out.

We returned to the ice palace at 2.30 p.m., thirty-one and a half hours after setting out. The cave was empty and we discovered from a note in the kitchen that the others had only just left:

Mon. 22nd Jan. 11 a.m.

Dear Stephen & Brian,
Hope very much that you have had success on Mt Carse and that the weather has not been too unkind. Lindsay and I got up Mt Kling with some difficulty at the end and bagged a 'Pt 5000' on the way down.

We are off to Royal Bay now with the sledge, on which we are taking as much as possible. We've left a few things for you and you'll need to bring 4 or 5 wands. I didn't want to remove any existing inward marker poles with you still on the glacier. We have taken the rubbish but could you do the final burn of what is actually in the cave?

See you soonest Royal Bay.
Best wishes from all,
Julian

PS: Remember the tripod – the head is with us. Kees.

Their sledge was a makeshift affair improvised from the remaining pair of skis and they had decided generously to set off with the bulk of the luggage, leaving the few remaining scraps of food for us. While we were relaxing back at the cave, they were ploughing down the Ross Glacier through hideous slushy snow, as Julian recalls: 'The journey turned out to be extremely tedious. The sledge started falling to pieces and balling up in front with slushy snow and by the time we were level with Helicopter Depot we had had enough. But we managed to continue, turning north towards the other side of the glacier. Lindsay suddenly disappeared up to his shoulders into a crevasse. Kees and I set to and hoisted him out with surprising ease and were in the process of sorting out ourselves and the sledge when Kees also disappeared into a gaping hole. Having got him out, I headed off in the only remaining direction and instantly plunged into another chasm.'

They managed to get clear of the minefield but eventually gave up on the hopeless sledge, dumping it to be collected later. It was dusk by the time they reached the lower glacier depot and a wet snow storm greeted them as they made their way in the dark back round the coast to Moltke Harbour, reaching the hut at midnight.

Brian and I came down the next morning. I am ashamed to say that the remaining rubbish was just burnt and left in the cave. Brian, the glaciologist, assured me that the blackened remains would eventually be crushed deep inside the Brögger Glacier as it slid year by year down towards the sea. Now all our plans were directed towards the northern side of the Allardyce Range; but, as Brian pointed out, there was a faint possibility that we might in an emergency find ourselves retreating through a storm down this southern side of the range. So we left the marker wands in place and filled in the front door with snow masonry, safely sealing the ice palace.

It felt rather sad to say goodbye to the desirable residence on the Ross Pass which had been our home for twenty-three days. The last we saw of it was a mournful column of black smoke rising from the chimney hole on the plateau. Then we heaved on our monstrously heavy rucksacks and headed off into the wind.

The weather was deteriorating rapidly and we had a foul descent, with the skis lurching and sticking in the warm slush. I cursed myself for not bringing wax but was still glad of the skis, safely bridging all the newly opened crevasses which had given the others such a hard time. After a long struggle it was a marvellous to reach the lower depot, leave skis and plastic boots to be collected later, and put on soft leather boots for the final snowless part of the descent.

Brian ran on ahead while I hung around to eat some scraps of food. Then I too started down the moraine to Little Moltke Harbour. As I descended I began to hear the sea roaring with a new intensity. Then I saw that it was not just water. The whole shoreline was clogged with a great belt of ice – hundreds of thousands of tons of brash ice driven back on to the shore by three days' easterly winds, grinding and gnashing in the surf. But just above the beach there was colour – luminous patches of yellow-green and russet moss, incredibly vivid after three and a half weeks' absence – and, as I descended the last few hundred feet to the beach, the unmistakable trumpeting sound of penguins.

11

Sörling Valley

So we returned to the sea, profoundly happy that at the last moment we had achieved something significant. As well as Vogel Peak and other assorted bumps and nunataks, our twenty-three-day sojourn at the ice palace had resulted finally in first ascents of Mt Kling and Mt Carse. The expedition could be deemed a success. We hoped to climb other peaks further north, but if we were successful they would be a bonus. For the moment I was happy just to be back at the coast, returning to life at high summer.

After a rest day we went back up to the Ross Glacier to collect the equipment on the abandoned sledge. It was a day of foul blizzing and I was glad that afternoon to get back down to the relative calm of Royal Bay. Walking back round Moltke Harbour I saw young gentoo penguins down at the beach for the first time, standing in huddles beside the water, eyeing the waves nervously on this first outing to the seaside. One youngster was trying to imitate the adults' trumpeting, raising its head high and squeaking bravely, but unable yet to master the powerful pulsing of the adults' diaphragms.

As I waded through the river, the parents were gathering up the young to herd them back up the valley, with all the other adults heading purposefully home like the commuters on Waterloo Bridge. Gentoo colonies are nearly always sited back from the sea and this one was about 200 yards up the gently sloping valley; but later that week, as we began ferrying equipment back north, we found a bigger colony much further from the coast.

The return to Cumberland Bay took ten days, in four stages, with an interim base halfway at the St Andrew's Bay hut. This time we took a slightly more direct route between Royal and St Andrew's Bays which brought us straight past the large gentoo colony. All the adults had gone off fishing, leaving about 200 youngsters to fend for themselves. From their flattened hillside patch, a path descended at least 600 feet over a distance of about half a mile to the sea. Every time the parents returned from the ocean, waddling ashore on stumpy legs with wings held out for balance, they had to climb laboriously all the way up that long hill.

While we relayed equipment back round the coast, Kees was also filming. Now that we had achieved our official climbing objectives, completing the film was our overriding aim. Although Kees was keen to portray the human side of the story, he knew and we knew that the wild inhabitants of South Georgia were the real stars. We became extras, walking with rucksacks and incongruous ski sticks along the shingle at St Andrew's Bay, swallowed up in a great tide of king penguins, briefly outraged, then indifferent as we passed on.

Although I liked the modest, unassuming, quietly-getting-on-with-my-own-business nature of the gentoos, the kings were altogether more entertaining. They would stand and wait as we approached, then shuffle back at the last minute, circling on their heels with heads held high in indignation, finally breaking ranks and escaping, all dignity abandoned as they ran away or belly-flopped to the ground to propel themselves horizontally across the shingle. We often surprised them asleep, standing with head tucked under a wing, or lying on the ground: to stand up, the prone penguin places the tip of its beak firmly on the ground and uses it as a stick to lever itself upright and start the indignant heel-shuffling routine.

At St Andrew's Bay there was always, day and night, the sound of trumpeting. It was rarely in unison and was often the work of a single bird, largely ignored by its neighbours, raising its beak to the sky with loud joyful abandon, then bowing its head low as the pulsating diaphragm came to rest. As well as these solo performers, most of them promenading along the beach, there was the background hubbub of squawking from the main rookery, set further back from the sea.

I visited the rookery on my last morning at St Andrew's Bay.

Kees woke me with a shout to say that the light was fantastic for photography. He was already out there, striding down to the beach with tripod and Aaton, determined to get the definitive film shot of dark figures on the grey sand bars, beaked heads silhouetted in a conversation piece against the sea, lit by silver and bronze shafts breaking through a great weight of black cloud.

It was beautiful but bitterly cold, particularly after I had waded through the Heaney Glacier meltstream to get to the rookery. The dawn had lost its first brilliance and I was sorely tempted to return to bed. But I was due to return to Cumberland Bay that day and I wanted my own rookery photos so I persevered, going in amongst the nesting birds to kneel down and take slow exposures in the faint dawn light, fighting to control my shivering and keep numb fingers functioning.

I have rarely seen such a dismal sight. There was no play of light on sky and water here: just thousands of birds, hunched on the mud at two-foot intervals, coats beaded with the night's rain, beaks jabbing angrily at neighbours. I stepped as delicately as possible between the birds but got several jabs. They also struck out with their powerful wings, battering hard against my shins. The din was appalling, the poultry farm smell was overwhelming, the birds all appeared identical and I wondered how on earth a spouse, when it returns from fishing to take a turn with the egg, can possibly find its mate. After all, during the initial courtship rituals, which include the presentation of ceremonial stones to prospective spouses, it is not uncommon for a suitor to find himself propositioning a bird of the same sex. Somehow though, once a heterosexual relationship has been established, a nest procured and an egg produced, the couple maintains a successful monogamous partnership amidst the clamour and apparent confusion.

King parents share the job of incubating, each taking turns to stand, sometimes for several days on end, with the large white egg balanced on top of its feet and further insulated by the characteristic belly flap. The only other penguin to incubate this way is the emperor, which lives much further south, where it has to protect its egg from the searing cold of permanent ice. The king, nesting mainly on the sub-Antarctic islands where there is ice-free ground, would appear to have no need for such elaborate procedures. The most convincing explanation for this unnecessary performance is that the king once also lived on the Antarctic ice and never lost the habit.

It is not just the egg which is kept in a pouch. The first chicks were now hatching and I could hear the high-pitched cheeping of a newly born king peeping out from under its parent's flap. Soon the parent bent over and gently pushed with its tapered beak, working the chick back to where it belonged as if ashamed of this ugly, grey, reptilian travesty of its own gleaming splendour.

No one knows exactly how many kings live at St Andrew's Bay. In 1925 the Grytviken manager estimated 1,100 birds. In 1936–7 Dr Brian Roberts counted about 700 adults. Counts between 1972 and 1974 revealed a total population of 6–7000, including chicks. But Cindy Buxton, after spending an entire summer here in 1982, thought that there were many more:

> I personally never counted the king penguins at St Andrew's Bay ... but I am quite convinced that during the height of the season, January and February, there were 50,000 king penguins scattered around the bay. This figure included the breeding birds, the previous season's chicks and the non-breeding birds. I would estimate there were between 15,000 and 20,000 nests at the colony ...

The latest BAS estimates put the island's total king population at about 100,000, with about 35,000 birds at St Andrew's Bay. Whatever the precise figure is, there has clearly been a huge population increase since the ravages of mass slaughter of the last century. Hundreds of thousands of penguins all around the Southern Ocean were killed to fuel the sealers' fires, or thrown into the trypots and rendered for additional blubber oil. The whalers brought a more sophisticated industry and killed only those birds they wanted to eat – succulent albatross chicks, taken straight from the nest, and the South Georgia pintail, shot more sportingly on the wing. Niall Rankin reported that before the whalers came flocks of 100 or more of these little ducks had been common on South Georgia. Now it is rare to see more than two at a time, and during our walks between St Andrew's Bay and Cumberland East Bay I only saw the occasional shy pair, usually lying low in the tussock.

On the last day of January Julian and I returned to the hut on Cumberland East Bay that we had left seven weeks earlier. The skua chick, which had been a little ball of fluff when we left, was now nearly as big as its parents. It still could not fly and ran around on the ground like a demented guinea fowl, bleating pathetically.

I was looking forward to our final spell here, at the idyllic Sörling Valley hut, so it was rather a shock as I walked round a bluff to discover boats pulled up on the beach, then a row of tents and rifles leaning against the hut.

A patrol had bumped into Julian and Kees at St Andrew's Bay a few days earlier – our first contact for forty-six days. They had radioed to a relieved Matt O'Hanlon, to tell him that SOMEX was making its way uninjured back to Sörling Valley. I had assumed that they would now be back at King Edward Point but here they were, still on our side of the bay, looking very disgruntled. I asked one of the squaddies if they were the lot sent to look for us. He gave me a look of profound boredom and muttered, 'We're fucking shipwrecked.'

John, the Royal Marines coxswain, explained that there was trouble with all the outboard motors, so that he now had several rigid raider boats stuck on the wrong side of Cumberland East Bay, along with eight bored young soldiers. That night they could see the lights of the *Society Explorer* at anchor seven miles away, where the rest of the garrison had been invited on board for a party. We could also see the huge bulk of a Russian vessel, the *Akademik Knipovich*, a research vessel doubling as the factory coordinator of a large fishing fleet operating in the area. The Cold War was still not officially over and the ship had satellite contact with Moscow, so John stuck scrupulously to security codes when he radioed King Edward Point. Matt was always addressed as Alpha Zero, there was much reference to 'our location', the boat problem was covered by various euphemisms and the Russian ship was always 'the other party'.

It was ironic that outboard motors, the Achilles heel that had plagued the 1982 SBS operations during the recces in this bay and Stromness Bay, should once again upset British operations on South Georgia. The problem was sorted out but first we shared Sörling Valley for three days with the marooned soldiers, who were clearly longing to get back to the bright lights of King Edward Point. Even after they left we remained in close contact with the garrison, keeping twice daily radio schedules to Matt, who was determined now to keep tabs on us. After seven weeks' complete isolation we were being drawn back into the world and already there was talk of arrangements for our passage back to the Falklands. The *Society Explorer* left, then a few days later we saw the huge pale shape of the *Europa* cruise liner off Grytviken. It looked quite surreal, then I thought what a sight it must have been in 1982 when *Queen Elizabeth II* and the *Canberra* had anchored in Cumberland East Bay, amongst a throng of warships.

One day John came back across the bay with fresh oranges, a packet of bacon, cigarettes, a case of Guinness and, most precious of all, our mail. Every fortnight a Hercules flies from the Falklands with newspapers and mail for the garrison, parachuting the parcels into Cumberland East Bay for collection by boat. On one drop that year the parachute failed to open and the bundle hit the water with such force that some of the letters were soaked. On another occasion a violent katabatic squall sent a parcel winging upwards before it came down way off course. Luckily all the drops were eventually recovered and we now had the luxury of sitting down to the two months' backlog.

It was a beautiful day – the best we ever had on the island – and we should really have been climbing, but we were far happier sitting in the sun with a cigarette and a can of Guinness, savouring every word from home. Rosie's four letters spoke with increasing gloom about the most disastrous winter on record in the Alps. Week after week with no snow, just bare earth, rain and ice . . . and every week a new batch of disgruntled skiers to deal with. So much for my Christmas card vision of snowbound Alps.

Julian discovered that he had featured in some glossy magazine's list of eligible batchelors, much to the annoyance of his long-suffering Elaine. He also had, from John Blashford-Snell, our 'honorary director', a bundle of Sunday papers – all from the same date, covering the full spectrum from the respectables to *News of the World*, complete with lurid revelations from Panama: *Inside Noriega's Palace of Evil — Photos that lift the lid on a kinky tyrant's amazing house of sin*. I was looking forward increasingly to returning home and seeing Rosie again, but it did also seem that we were better off out of the world, however, artificial and indulgent our escape might be.

The letters, the newspapers and the supplies from the garrison all softened our isolation. It seems to be a problem with modern expeditions that we rely increasingly on home props to screen ourselves from and colour our experience of the wild. One day, doing my last of four load ferries from Hound Bay, growing slightly tired of the long walk up Sörling Valley, I resorted to the vulgar excess of travelling to music, plugged into my Walkman. Bach's Mass in B Minor seemed an appropriate choice, with the Kyrie Eleison blasting through my head as the skuas divebombed; then, an hour later, an extraordinary sequence of chords from the Credo as I gazed out over the blue, green and purple of Hound Bay to a distant luminescent iceberg; then, walking round the beach, the glorious Sanctus, with its relentless descending bass buttressing the soaring flight of sopranos and trumpets, making you believe that there must be a heaven.

Of course it was an over-indulgent feast of the senses, doing justice neither to Bach nor to South Georgia, and for most of that last fortnight I was content just to enjoy the island on its own terms. At the end of our letter-reading session I walked up to the bluff above the hut where a giant petrel, the ugly yellow-eyed 'stinker' sat beside its downy white chick. At first the mother objected, but soon I was allowed to sit and photograph only three feet from the nest, while mother and bird sat panting in the unaccustomed heat. On other occasions I went to the light-mantled sooty albatross nest, poised on a great wobbling clump of tussock halfway up the cliff. The chick already sat a foot high, but apart from its well defined face, beak and flippers, it remained an almost featureless ball of grey fluff, with no hint of the parents' soaring grace as they skimmed over the clifftops in an aerial ballet that would keep me entranced for hours.

Sörling Valley also had its sounds: the burbling of the stream where we washed and the heavier swell of the seashore, sometimes shattered by the distant roar of the Nordenskjöld Glacier 'calving' a great block of ice into the bay and sending little tidal waves surging towards us; the soft thud of reindeer hooves, the belching of the last few elephants that had not gone to sea; the angry chatter of Antarctic terns, the haunting cry of the albatross, rather like a peacock's wail, but with a strange echo as it drew breath; and, every night as we settled down in hut and tents, the massed squeaking of hundreds of rats, the stowaways that came eighty years ago with the whalers, scurrying out from their burrows in the tussock.

Of all the sounds we lived with perhaps the commonest, during our walks around the Barff Peninsula, was the sudden growl of a fur seal, rearing up from behind a rock or clump of tussock. One morning Julian and I walked a few miles round the coast from the hut and stopped every few minutes to watch the seals sunbathing, sleeping, chasing each other across the beach or playing in the water, rolling and diving in a languid ballet against a backdrop of blue ice and white mountains. Of course they were enchanting, but what made their ubiquitous presence so poignant was the knowledge that only seventy years earlier the fur seal had been thought extinct.

As James Weddell recorded, the earlier raiders had hunted the fur seal to the edge of extinction by 1822. Sporadic catches continued until 1907, when the American sealer Benjamin Cleveland came on the *Daisy* to clean up all the remaining animals he could find, with blatant contempt for the sealing ordinances. After that people assumed that the fur seal was extinct, until the 1930s when the research ship, RRS *Discovery*, reported rare sightings of fur seals at remote spots on South Georgia's shore. By the 1940s it was common knowledge that the fur seal was certainly not extinct; nevertheless numbers remained small. In 1947 Niall Rankin was excited to discover fur seal ears in the stomach of a leopard seal. A few weeks later he found and photographed a whole colony of live fur seals, but when he published *Antarctic Isle* the following year he was careful not to describe the exact location of the colony. Nigel Bonner was the first biologist to investigate the seals thoroughly. During his first spell on South Georgia, from

1953 to 1955, he was based at the Bay of Isles with Bernard Stonehouse, working mainly on penguins. But he was aware of the fur seals and in 1956 borrowed a sealing vessel to land at Bird Island, where he found a breeding colony with about 4,000 pups.

Bonner's theory is that a few seals survived the ravages of the nineteenth century, hidden away on the isolated coast of Willis Island – named after Captain Cook's 'wild and drinking midshipman' who was the first on board *Resolution* to sight land – right at the western tip of South Georgia. The seals gradually multiplied, then ran out of space and moved across to the more commodious Bird Island. In 1958 Bonner erected the first little hut on Bird Island and started biological research there. Later a bigger hut was built and there is now a proper field station, the only British Antarctic Survey base still operating in South Georgia.

The fur seals soon moved back to the main island, re-establishing themselves right along the coast and it is now estimated that there are 1,500,000 of them based on South Georgia. One of the ironic things about the story of this animal, hunted mercilessly by man, is that its recent dramatic revival may have been enhanced directly by man's even more profitable slaughter of the whales. Nothing has been proved, but many scientists believe that with perhaps 90 per cent of the baleen whales now gone from the Southern Ocean, there must be a huge surplus of krill available for smaller krill-eaters like the fur seals. This ecological irony was illustrated most poignantly at the little bay of Ocean Harbour on the east coast of the Barff Peninsula.

It was a lovely walk to Ocean Harbour, climbing gently up a 'Scottish' glen with its water-nourished emerald ribbons of moss, over a pass and down to a perfect natural harbour, folded deep in the hills with the arms of rock guarding the entrance. The land at the head of the bay was littered with the eerie remains of a small whaling station that operated here from 1909 to 1919 – shattered buildings, old foundations, rotting floor joists, a mini-gauge railway, cast iron boilers collapsed like drunken pot-bellied giants on the grass, and a huge steam winch stamped with the logo of R. Rogers & Co. Limited, Stockton-on-Tees. The view out of the bay was dominated by the three masts of an iron-hulled sailing ship, the *Bayard*. Even in this apparently sheltered harbour she ripped her moorings in 1911 and ran aground on the southern shore of the bay, where she rests, rusted to a mellow patina, with cormorants nesting in the tussock grass that now festoons her bowsprit.

On the shore beside the hulk there were scores of fur seals gambolling, sparring and barking in an exuberant affirmation of life. Their playground was a field of bones – huge white bones, piled like driftwood on the beach. They were mainly ribs, like great curved spars, but also vertebrae, each the size of a large log, and occasional skulls, some standing almost as tall as a man. When Rankin photographed Ocean Harbour in 1947 the whale bone were strewn much more thickly on the beach. Since then many have been washed out to sea, but there still remains a poignant killing field, dating from that most profligate early phase of the southern whaling industry, when most of the whale's carcass was thrown away unused.

Three times during the last phase of the expedition we attempted another major climb. We set our sights on Mt Roots, named after Walter Roots, the ski-mountaineer on Carse's first expedition. It was now, after our recent ascent of Kling, the last major unclimbed peak in the Allardyce Range. This time there was to be no extended subterranean siege – just a quick dash up the Nordenskjöld Glacier to an overnight camp below the peak, followed by a single push up the North Face.

Our first attempt was on February 6th. Lindsay, Brian, Julian and I walked up on a beautiful afternoon to pitch the large tent on the ice just below the peak. All we achieved was a day of waiting through cloud and intermittent drizzle, followed by a grateful retreat on the 8th. On the 12th we went up again with new supplies. Just as we got the tent pitched it was hit by what I dismissed as 'just a williewaw blowing down the glacier'. The williewaws multiplied and the storm blew all night with the strongest gusts we had experienced since Boxing Day. Lindsay had the misfortune to be on the windward side and spent the night as a human tentpole, propping up the bucking tent. We abandoned the attempt the following afternoon.

Back at the Sörling Valley hut, Alpha Zero informed us over the radio that he wanted us ready for evacuation to King Edward

Point by February 20th. On the 17th the weather looked moderately hopeful, so we set off for one last attempt on Mt Roots. This time Kees came too, determined to get some artistic footage of the Magnificent Four hopping in procession across the Nordenskjöld crevasses, backlit by dazzling afternoon sunshine. For the third time we pitched the tent at the same spot on the upper glacier just as the clouds started to pour over the Allardyce Range. This time it snowed heavily all night and all the next day as the five of us lay low, stacked up like a pod of elephant seals in the three-man tent.

Providence clearly intended that Mt Roots should remain inviolate, but we did get some excellent film footage of the sort of authentic details so often missing from mountain films: bleak shots from outside of snow pouring steadily down on the tent; inside, nice cameos of Brian making yet another cup of tea, for want of anything better to do; Lindsay lost in silent communion with his barometer; me reading my second novel of the day. However, Kees got the best footage the next morning when we packed up to leave, grimacing as the snow beat against our faces and we fought the tent into sodden rucksacks before setting off, blind leading the blind, stumbling through a minefield of crevasses half-concealed under nine inches of new snow. Brian rose splendidly to the occasion, volunteering at one stage to fall into a crevasse and be saved by Julian's adroit rope-handling. Kees got the shots, but without sound; so once we were down off the glacier he asked Brian and Julian to perform again for the Dog. 'We must make it realistic . . . that you say something.'

'But you don't say anything when you fall in a slot.'

'But we have to have a reaction . . . that we understand this is something dramatic.'

'Well, I suppose . . . I don't know . . . perhaps you might shout out "Oh shit!" or something like that.'

'All right. And Julian – you must shout that you have him safe on the rope.'

So Kees adjusted the recording levels and held up the soggy Dog while Brian stood there on the shore of Cumberland East Bay, in the falling snow, shouting over and over again, with every possible inflection he could muster, 'Oh shit!', followed each time by

Julian, like some triumphant deep-sea fisherman, yelling 'Got you!'

Back at the hut the next morning, February 20th, a message came through on the radio that two rigid raiders would come over to collect us 'at 14.30 hours from your location'. We had a busy morning packing barrels and rucksacks, cleaning the hut, burning the last of the rubbish, flattening the blackened remains and burying them deep, to rot in the acid peat. The two boats arrived on schedule and we said goodbye to Sörling Valley. By tea-time we were wallowing in hot baths at King Edward Point.

12

Autumn and Spring

During our last few days on South Georgia I did my best to destroy the benefits of eleven weeks' healthy living in the wild. At King Edward Point there were still plentiful cigarettes, cases of beer, several remaining bottles of whisky and an almost limitless supply of videos. I reached my nadir one afternoon with a film called *Death Wish IV* (or was it *Death Wish V?*).

Lindsay and Brian were more healthy, disappearing for long walks in the hills around Grytviken. Often they went independently and Lindsay, returning from another lonely wander, would look happier than he had ever done cooped up with the rest of us. It was like our first expedition, to Afghanistan twelve years earlier, when he left the rest of us and returned three days later from a cathartic solo climb, singing for joy and completely at peace with the world. People talk about the camaraderie and closeness of expeditions, but often it is more a case of working together in an atmosphere of mutual tolerance, keeping close friendships for home.

Our expedition was gently winding down with the Austral autumn and in the absence of any dramatic denouement my thoughts were turning increasingly to home. It was also, mindless videos notwithstanding, a time for reflection. Living at King Edward Point as guests of the British Army, looking across the Cove to the rusty ruins and white church at Grytviken, one was prompted inevitably to ponder man's incongruous presence on the island and his future both on South Georgia and in the whole of Antarctica.

Our little adventure would never have happened without the support of the armed services, authorised at a very high level.

Their generous hospitality had been overwhelming and at the end of the garrison's four-month tour, when the men's nerves were frayed and they were longing to get home, they still made us welcome at Shackleton House. Yet for all the hospitality, one was bound to ask what the army was doing there in the first place. Is Britain just making a very expensive point about sovereignty, determined to save face after the 1982 debacle? Or is there a genuine strategic advantage in hanging on?

If Britain is to continue a tradition now two-centuries old of taking a major role in Antarctic exploration, then the possession of islands on the very edge of Antarctica must be a boon. The official line of the Foreign and Commonwealth Office and of the British Antarctic Survey at the beginning of 1990 suggested that Britain not only intended to maintain a high profile in the area but was also considering very seriously the distant possibility of commercial exploitation of Antarctica. Along with several other signatories to the Antarctic Treaty, British representatives wanted to ratify CRAMRA – the Convention on Regulation of Antarctic Mineral Resource Activities. The proposal outlined a stringent set of safeguards to cover any mining or oil-drilling activities in the area – safeguards so stringent, said their proponents, that it could be many years before any mining or drilling became practical. However, the implicit philosophy seemed to be an admission of the possibility, even desirability, of minerals exploitation. If that exploitation were to take place, Britain's strategic sub-Antarctic islands like South Georgia, ice-free in summer and only occasionally affected by winter pack, could be a valuable staging post for commercial operations. In the event of international disputes leading to war, the military infrastructure established since 1982 would be ready in place.

That is probably an unduly cynical interpretation. The official enlightened view was put to a bristling Julian when we met Nigel Bonner at Port Stanley before Christmas. At present there was nothing in the Antarctic Treaty to stop anyone mining or drilling for offshore oil. The proposed Convention would seal that gap in the constitution. Not only did it lay down 'the most stringent set of environmental safeguards ever devised'; its framework also insisted on a consensus of Treaty members before any one member

155

would be allowed to start operations. In effect the Convention would lay so many difficulties in the path of prospective developers that they would never be able to start work. Above all, the Convention was an extension of the existing Antarctic Treaty system, which had protected the continent so well for the last thirty years.

In contrast to the wealth of scientific and diplomatic expertise backing CRAMRA, our expedition flag, proclaiming support for an 'Antarctic World Park' seemed on the face of it a woolly gesture of the amateur fringe. But the philosophy behind it must be the right one. Later, in Cambridge, I asked the Director of the British Antarctic Survey, David Drewry, why the Antarctic Treaty consultative parties could not go a stage further than CRAMRA and agree to a convention banning all commercial exploitation for all time. 'We'd love to do that,' he assured me, 'but some parties would never agree to it, at least not yet. For the moment CRAMRA is the best safeguard we can come up with.'

The Foreign and Commonwealth Office, supported by the British Antarctic Survey, was clinging stubbornly to CRAMRA, but already there were dissenters amongst the consultative parties. New Zealand and Australia had declared outright bans on mining in their Antarctic sectors. France, too, said she would not sign CRAMRA. These gestures could be dismissed as vote-catching gimmicks of governments jumping aboard the environmental bandwagon. France, in particular, with her record of nuclear devastation in the Pacific and the recent sabotage of the Greenpeace ship *Rainbow Warrior*, badly needed to score some environmental points. What better than a dramatic gesture in Antarctica, the ultimate 'Last Great Wilderness'?

Whatever their motivations, the ranks of the dissenters were swelling and at the Antarctic Treaty meeting in Santiago in November 1990 the consultative parties failed to ratify CRAMRA; not only that – they went a step further and decided at the next meeting to discuss a new protocol with comprehensive measures for the protection of the Antarctic environment.

Since then there have been dramatic developments. At the latest meeting, at Madrid in April 1991, the two camps agreed on a compromise which goes way beyond the dubious safeguards of

CRAMRA. One group of nations, led by Australia and France, were pushing for an indefinite prohibition on minerals activities in Antarctica, while Britain and the United States of America, after first opposing a permanent ban did, however, take a big step forward in agreeing to a fifty-year ban as part of a blueprint which provides the basis for a comprehensive environmental protection regime.

If ratified by the member governments, the new proposal will save Antarctica for the next generation. As for future generations, if after fifty years any Treaty member chooses to request a review, the minerals ban may only be lifted if three-quarters of the nations then voting, including all the present twenty-six voting nations, agree.

Many of the non-governmental World Park campaigners have suggested that Antarctica should be administered as a nature reserve by the United Nations. A few years ago the proposal would have been laughable; recent events suggest that the UN is actually capable of making and implementing decisions. However, the Antarctic Treaty may well remain the best forum for deciding the continent's future. From its elitist beginnings, the Treaty has swelled to twenty-six voting nations (those which actually have scientific bases on the continent) out of a total of thirty-nine, representing 80 per cent of the world's population. If its members continue to increase, if it continues to provide legislation making commercial exploitation to all intents and purposes impossible, and if its members continue to freeze, or ideally renounce, all sovereign claims on the continent, perhaps it really does offer the best hope.

Antarctica covers a tenth of the globe's surface. It is so vast that it seems almost impossible for man to make any impact at all. However, the unique, rich, varied wildlife is all concentrated around the coast and surrounding islands and it is in those tortuous waters, beset by icebergs, that any commercial development, in the form of oil drilling, would be most likely to happen. Even with the most stringent safeguards imaginable, the potential for disaster is terrifying. And if we need an example of exploitation run riot, what better illustration than the derelict ghost towns at Grytviken, Stromness, Husvik and Leith, or the relics at Ocean

Harbour – the rusting memorials to an industry that failed to control itself?

Commercial whaling has stopped in the South, although Norway, Iceland and Japan have recently threatened to renew minke hunting in the North. The southern seals are protected. As for minerals, the Shackleton Report of the 1970s stated that South Georgia, unlike Antarctica proper, has nothing valuable to offer and that offshore oil deposits are unlikely. However, the waters around South Georgia teem with fish. During the 1970s several species were drastically overfished. The Russians and Japanese have also experimented with krill harvests. Luckily, the red crustaceans are not very palatable for humans and so far it has not proved commercially attractive to convert the krill to animal feed on a large scale. But if the technology improved, perhaps we could see the Antarctic equivalent of the acre of Amazon forest destroyed to provide grazing for enough beef to make one hamburger. And if the krill stocks were wiped out, with them would go the entire Antarctic food chain.

Since 1982 all the nations fishing around Antarctica have signed a Convention for the Conservation of Antarctic Marine Living Resources (CCAMLR). Seals are protected by a separate convention. However, Nigel Bonner admitted during our conversation at Port Stanley that although the voluntary ethos of CCAMLR, 'is a fine philosophy, it has not worked perfectly in practice'. While we were on South Georgia, a BAS expert, Inigo Everson, visited the *Akademik Knipovich*, anchored in Cumberland East Bay. As far as he could tell, the Russians had stuck to agreed quotas, 'but each year they fight to get as high a quota as possible' – hardly surprising from a nation facing economic collapse and drastic food shortages. Everson would like to see much lower quotas being established in the first place.

South Georgia, unlike the Falklands, has no exclusion zone, but the Magistrate is empowered to charge harbour dues. At King Edward Point, Matt O'Hanlon told us that the fee paid during the 1989–90 season by the Russian factory ship heading a fishing fleet of eighteen boats was a paltry £800. The following year, however, a civilian harbourmaster was appointed – Caradoc Jones, the Welsh climber and marine biologist who did not make it to Tibet in 1987. He was responsible for implementing a charge of £1000 for every transhipment of fish in South Georgian waters. The money helps to finance continuing research, and collection of dues is a way of policing the fishing, keeping an eye on exactly what is being taken from the ocean. Perhaps that flexing of territorial muscle, in the interests of conservation, attempting to maintain a sustainable harvest, is a good justification for Britain's continued presence on the island. There were other hopeful signs. After several years' unsatisfactory sinking of rubbish in Cumberland East Bay, with some of it inevitably drifting over to the Barff Peninsula, just as we left the island the Royal Engineers were constructing a proper incinerator at King Edward Point. The Salvesen consultants were making provision for removing old oil from rusting storage tanks at the whaling stations. Amongst everyone visiting and working on the island there seemed to be an attitude that it was a precious place to be looked after. Perhaps, if we treat South Georgia more and more as an invaluable sanctuary, the same respect will permeate our cooperation with other states in the international territory of Antarctica itself.

Our expedition was one of a growing number of groups visiting the Antarctic regions for recreation. I would like to think that our impact was minimal but there were times, walking through the penguin colonies at St Andrew's Bay, when I wondered whether we should be there at all. There were only five of us, but the cruise ships bring groups of up to 500 passengers, with more potential for disturbing wildlife. Brian, visiting the Antarctic region this time as a tourist, said afterwards that he found it hard to justify. When he returns to the Antarctic mainland in 1992 it will be as a scientist, drilling ice cores to measure past air sulphur levels for comparison with his work on current levels around the world. He will be using Antarctica as the ultimate pristine laboratory.

The British Antarctic Survey is respected throughout the world for the quality of its research. Much of that research is extremely useful, such as the vital work on marine biology or the development of knowledge about global climate; but it can never be justified entirely in terms of pure usefulness or profit. Most field scientists would probably admit that they start from a sense of wonder and a desire for adventure that transcends such mundane criteria. In 1911 Apsley Cherry-Garrard, together with Wilson and Bowers, suffered unspeakable hardship travelling at the dead of winter to Cape Crozier for the ostensible purpose of collecting emperor penguin eggs, to examine the foetuses for evidence of an important evolutionary theory. Writing later in *The Worst Journey in the World* he concluded:

> And I tell you, if you have the desire for knowledge and the desire to give it physical expression, go out and explore. If you are a brave man you will do nothing. If you are fearful you may do much, for none but cowards have need to prove their bravery. Some will tell you that you are mad and nearly all will say, 'What's the use?' For we are a nation of shopkeepers and no shopkeeper will look at research which does not promise a fixed return within a year. And so you will sledge nearly alone. But those with whom you sledge will not be shopkeepers: that is worth a good deal. If you march your winter journey you will have your reward, so long as all you want is a penguin's egg.

Most scientists, explorers and climbers would probably distance themselves from the remarks about shopkeepers. After all it is the 'shopkeepers' who make possible the indulgence of Antarctic egg collecting or going to South Georgia to climb mountains, often directly sponsoring our adventures. But if one puts the apparent arrogance in the context of 1912, Cherry-Garrard's remarks are a good model for our attitude to wilderness. And Antarctica really is a wilderness. It is the only continent without an indigenous human population. Attempts at conservation do not face the hideous complexities of, say, the Himalaya, with its rapidly expanding local population. It is still possible to preserve this place of unique beauty, and even if the vast majority of us never even see it, we must be infinitely richer just for knowing that it is there.

Kees spent a busy last week at King Edward Point. He slaved for hours in the darkroom, making prints of the official garrison photograph for all the soldiers, by way of thanking them for all the help they had given SOMEX. He also had filming to do, getting additional poignant shots of the Grytviken whaling station and rigging up a highly effective 'cheat' shot to complete the snowcave sequence, filming each of us in the tent, pitched inside a warehouse to create the right subdued lighting. Lindsay, by far the best natural actor, surpassed himself in a reconstructed conversation with his barometer. Brian's crevasse sequence also needed additional detail, so we found a small slot on a tiny glacier above the Cove. Kees was lowered inside with the Aaton and when he was ready Brian leapt in after him, held on the rope by Lindsay, while I kicked down enough snow to suggest a treacherous collapsed bridge.

It was a beautiful afternoon with a rainbow arched across the turquoise expanse of Cumberland East Bay and I began to have pangs about leaving. Three days later, on a blue calm morning, the Royal Fleet Auxiliary ship *Diligence* steamed into King Edward Cove and we were asked to embark, while the garrison officers made the final arrangements for the changeover at King Edward Point. Along with the junior ranks we spent the next two days on a sightseeing trip to Stromness Bay. The weather remained absolutely perfect, with all the peaks arrayed in a crystal blue sky, now that we were powerless to climb them. They were still there, bathed in the translucent sunshine of an autumn afternoon, when we finally sailed on March 1st, escorted out to sea by squadrons of albatrosses.

Ten days later we returned to Britain, flying in over Oxfordshire. Julian stared gloomily down at the huge arable fields ploughed across the countryside, with hardly a tree or hedgerow left in sight. But at least, when he returned to Shropshire, he would be out there planting new woods, doing something useful for the land. Brian, too, had a specific job to return to and the next morning he would be back in his laboratory, while in London Kees would be looking through the first rushes of the film. For Lindsay and me the homecoming was more ambiguous, with no clearly defined jobs waiting for us, and my sense of returning to limbo was intensified by the knowledge that Rosie would still be in France for another two months.

My gloom deepened as the RAF bus took me through the cluttered countryside to Reading. Everywhere there seemed to be new charmless housing estates and ugly revamped theme pubs. At

Reading the train was late and then I had to change and wait at Swindon, surely the most desolate railway station in the whole world, particularly on a Sunday afternoon.

Bath at least was beautiful and I cheered up at last when the taxi deposited me and my luggage at the village of Larkhall. It was a balmy afternoon with a smell of blossom in the air and I suddenly realised that, just as my Antarctic summer was ending, an early spring had already arrived in the Northern Hemisphere. I dragged my luggage down the terrace but before going into the empty house I had a look in the garden. It was exactly fourteen weeks since the grey day we had planted our bulbs and there, pushing up through the earth, were the young furled leaves of 140 tulips.

Appendix I

Expeditions to South Georgia

1775 *First known landing* on South Georgia, by Captain Cook.

1786 *Start of sealing,* which was to be the main motivation for many nineteenth-century Antarctic voyages.

1882–3 *International Polar Year Expedition.* German scientific expedition based at Royal Bay.

1901–3 *Swedish Polar Expedition.* The main party, led by Otto Nordenskjöld, was involved in one of the great Antarctic epics on the mainland peninsula. Meanwhile, the expedition's ship, the *Antarctic,* captained by Carl Anton Larsen, carried out survey work on South Georgia.

1904 *The start of the whaling industry.* C. A. Larsen established the first whaling station at Grytviken. The whaling industry continued here, and at five other stations, ntil 1965.

1916 *Shackleton's Rescue Mission.* Shackleton's expedition had called at South Georgia in 1915, en route for the attempted Antarctic crossing. Eighteen months later Shackleton reappeared at Stromness, having survived the sinking of the *Endurance,* the trek to Elephant Island, the 800-

mile voyage from there in an open boat, followed by the first-ever crossing of South Georgia.

1928–9   *Kohl-Larsen Expedition.* Ludwig and Margit Kohl-Larsen made some of the first explorations of the island's interior, in particular the huge glacier plateau named after them.

1946–7   *Niall Rankin's Ornithological Expedition.*

1951–7   *The South Georgia Surveys.* Four expeditions organised privately and led by *Duncan Carse*. Helped generously by sealing boat crews, Carse was able to land at points all round the island and set off on prolonged sledging journeys, making a comprehensive survey of the interior.

1954–5   *British South Georgia Expedition.* George Sutton led the first actual mountaineering expedition to the island. The only major peak climbed was Brooker, but much useful exploration was achieved.

1961   *Duncan Carse's solo sojourn* at Undine South Harbour. An experiment in living alone. Carse's hut was smashed by a freak surge wave, after which he had to live alone for 116 days in a tent, before making contact with a sealing ship.

1964–5   *British Joint Services Expedition.* First ascents of Mt Paget and Mt Sugartop. Detailed survey of Royal Bay area.

1968   Ice patrol vessel HMS *Endurance* comes into operation.

1969   *British Antarctic Survey* (BAS) begins operating at King Edward Point.

1980   *French Yacht 'Basile'*. Second ascent of Mt Paget
                and the first from the north – from Nordenskjöld
                Glacier.

1981–2   *British Joint Services Expedition*. From a base at
                Royal Bay, the expedition made the second ascent
                of Mt Brooker, crossed the Ross Pass and
                repeated Carse's sledging route to Drygalski Fjord.
                An attempt on Mt Carse was defeated by bad
                weather.

1982   *Argentinian Occupation of King Edward Point.*
                Cindy Buxton and Annie Price's penguin survey at St
                Andrew's Bay.

1985–6   *New Zealand Expedition*. From a base at Royal
                Bay, scientific work was done and minor peaks
                climbed.

1988   *Christian de Marliave* ('Criquet') landed at St
                Andrew's Bay by *Damien II* and made solo first
                ascent of Nordenskjöld in just two days.

1989–90   *Southern Ocean ountaineering Expedition*. First
                ascents of Vogel Peak, Mt Kling and Mt Carse.

1991   *Caradoc Jones* (the South Georgia harbourmaster)
                with Capt Ian Mills of the Royal Marines made
                the third ascent of Mt Paget, climbing the North-
                East Ridge from the Nordenskjöld Glacier.

For a comprehensive history of all but the most recent
expeditions to the island, see *The Island of South Georgia*
by Robert Headland.

Appendix II
Acknowledgments

The Southern Ocean Mountaineering Expedition would like to thank all the many institutions and individuals who made possible such a memorable adventure:

Financial Support

Barclays Bank
British Mountaineering Council (Sports Council Grant)
Mr Peter Clarke
Colonel Henry Day
Kronospan
Mercury Rowan Mullens Ltd
Mount Everest Foundation

Equipment and Supplies

Bernard Matthews	Pre-cooked meals
Bowater Industries	Harcostar plastic storage drums
Camera Care Systems	Camera cases
Daniel Quiggin & Son	Chocolate-coated Kendal Mint Cake
First Ascent	Asolo boots, Thermarest sleeping mats
John Gau Productions	Kodak 16 mm cine film stock
John West	Tinned fish, fruit and vegetables
Karrimor	Baltoro & Alpiniste protective clothing
Kodak	Kodachrome, Ektar and Tmax still film
Marks & Spencer	Champagne, wine and assorted groceries
Matthew Gloag & Son	Famous Grouse whisky
MD Foods	Samsoe cheese

Mountain Equipment	Down sleeping bag and Goretex windsuit
Mountain Technology	Ice axes and snow stakes
Pietro Negroni	Salami and Parma ham
Rowntree Mackintosh	Yorkie bars
Simmers Biscuits	Ginger biscuits and oatcakes
Taymar	Epigas butane/propane mix
W. H. Smith	Books
Wild Country	Goretex mittens, tents
Zanzibar Productions	Aaton 16 mm film camera and accessories

Transport, Accommodation and Administrative Support

His Excellency, W. H. Fullerton, Governor of the Falkland Islands, and Mrs Fullerton.
General Paul Stevenson CBE, Commander of British Forces in the Falkland Islands, and Mrs Stevenson.
Captain Norman Hodgson RN, the officers and crew of HMS *Endurance*.
Major Matthew O'Hanlon, Commander of the South Georgia garrison. The Royal Marines, the Royal Engineers and the Green Howards.
Captain David Pet, the officers and crew of RNFA *Diligence*.

And the other people who helped so generously to make the expedition possible, with apologies for any unintentional omissions

Mr Norman Abbot, Mrs Meg Arrol, Captain Nicholas Barker RN, Colonel John Blashford-Snell CBE, Major Anthony Bleakeley, Mr Christopher Bontein, Mr Chris Bradley, Ms Geraldine Buckley, Mr Duncan Carse CBE, Lord Chorley, Mr Cochrane, Mr Matt Dickinson, Mr Chris Dunbabin, General Patrick Fagan MBE, Ms Elaine Fraser, Mr Hamish Fulton, Mr John Gau, Captain Ian Gemmell, Mr John Greyburn, Ms Rosie Grieves-Cook, Mrs Jan Griffin, Mr and Mrs Griffith, Snr Giuseppe Gorradi, The Earl and Countess of Gowrie, Mr Peter

Holloway, Mr Luke Hughes, Mr Martin Kaindle, Colonel Douglas Keelan, Major Brian Kerslake, Mr David Lamb, Mr David Lyon, Mr Hamish McDougall, Ms Kirsty McGill, Mrs E. Mostyn-Owen, The Hon. Janet Needham, Mr John Netherwood, Ms Jackie Palmer-Jones, Mr I. Parris, Captain Pat Parsons, Mr Lars Poulsen, Mr Tom Price, Mr John Robson, Mr Bill Ruthven, Ms Siobhan Sheridan, Ms Cally Southern, Mr John Stevenson, Ms Ruth Townsend, Mr Alan Tritton, Sergeant John Twist, Mr Rodney Tyler, Dr Mark Upton, Sergeant Neil West, Ms Joe Williams, Captain Tug Wilson, Mr Nigel de N. Winser.

Appendix III
Select Bibliography

Cindy Buxton, *Survival South Atlantic*, London, Granada Publishing, 1983

Apsley Cherry-Garrard, *The Worst Journey in the World*, London, Chatto & Windus, 1965

Robert Headland, *The Island of South Georgia*, Cambridge University Press, 1984

Roland Huntford, *Shackleton*, London, Hodder & Stoughton, 1985

Frank Hurley, *Argonauts of the South*, New York, G. P. Putnam's Sons, 1925.

Otto Nordenskjöld, J. G. Andersson and C. A. Larsen, *Antarctica, or Two Years amongst the Ice of the South Pole*, Hurst & Blackett, 1905 (facsimile: London, C. Hurst & Co, 1977)

Wilfrid Noyce and Ian McMorrin (eds), *The World Atlas of Mountaineering*, Nelson, 1969

Roger Perkins, *Operation Paraquat*, Bath, Picton Publishing, 1986

Niall Rankin, *Antarctic Isle, Wildlife in South Georgia*, London, Collins, 1951

Ernest Shackleton, *South*, London, Heinemann, 1919

Geoffrey Sutton, *Glacier Island, the Official Record of the British South Georgia Expedition, 1954–55*, London, Chatto & Windus, 1957

Frank Worsley, *Shackleton's Boat Journey*, London, Hodder & Stoughton, 1940 (Folio Society, 1974)

Index